Baby Blues® **10** Scrapbook

threats, &bribes & videotape

threats, &bribes, videotape

by Rick Kirkman & Jerry Scott

Andrews McMeel
Publishing®

Kansas City • Sydney • London

Andrews McMeel Publishing, LLC
an Andrews McMeel Universal company
1130 Walnut Street, Kansas City, Missouri 64106

www.andrewsmcmeel.com

ISBN: 978-0-8362-6750-1

Library of Congress Control Number: 9885358

To Kim and Abbey, the loves of my life.

—J.S.

Once again, for Sukey, who deserves more recognition than this.

To my Mom and Dad, tireless promoters of my work.

And thanks to the members of the National Cartoonists Society for
the last decade of inspiration, encouragement, and hospitality.

—R.K.

BABY BLUES

BY RICK KIRKMAN / JERRY SCOTT

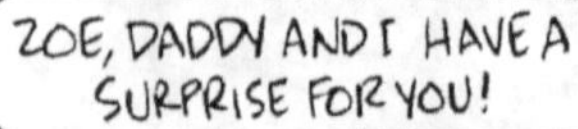

ZOE, DADDY AND I HAVE A SURPRISE FOR YOU!

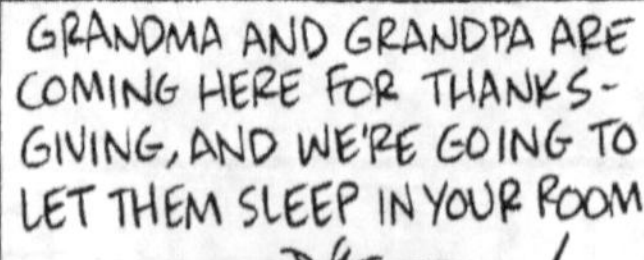

GRANDMA AND GRANDPA ARE COMING HERE FOR THANKSGIVING, AND WE'RE GOING TO LET THEM SLEEP IN YOUR ROOM!

AND THAT MEANS YOU GET TO SLEEP ON THE FLOOR IN HAMMIE'S ROOM! WON'T THAT BE GREAT??

HOW WAS THAT?
A LITTLE TOO ENTHUSIASTIC... TRY SMILING WITHOUT SHOWING YOUR MOLARS.

ZOE! GRANDMA AND GRANDPA ARE HERE!
YAY!!!

GWANDMA! GWANDPA!
THERE'S MY GIRL!
HI, SWEETHEART!

POP! I TOLD YOU NOT TO BRING HER ANY CANDY!

I KNOW, BUT I THOUGHT ONE PIECE WOULD BE OKAY...
I WIKE HIM!

MO' CANDY, GWANDPA?
HEE-HEE! SURE!
POP, THAT'S THE FIFTH PIECE OF CANDY SHE'S HAD THIS MORNING!

WELL, KIDS WILL BE KIDS...
YEAH, BUT I WOULDN'T WANT HER TO OVERDO IT, AND...UH... I DID ASK YOU TO TAKE IT EASY...SO...

WHACK!
PUT THE CANDY AWAY, MAC!

OKIE-DOKIE.
THE OLDER THEY GET, THE LESS TACTFUL YOU HAVE TO BE.
I'LL REMEMBER THAT.

MOM?...POP? WHY DON'T WE ALL JOIN HANDS FOR THE BLESSING?

OOF!
ERK!
AGH!
UNHH!

ON SECOND THOUGHT, MAYBE WE DIDN'T NEED TO PUT ALL THREE LEAVES IN THE TABLE...
HURRY UP AND PRAY, SON! MY SHOULDERS ARE GOING NUMB!
KIRKMAN & SCOTT

I WONDER IF WANDA NEEDS ANY HELP WITH THE DISHES?
I DOUBT IT...YOUR MOTHER IS IN THERE.

I WONDER IF SHE NEEDS ANY HELP WITH THE KIDS?
I DOUBT IT...YOUR MOTHER IS IN THERE.

KIRKMAN & SCOTT

I WONDER IF SHE NEEDS ANY HELP WITH MOM?
NOW THAT'S A POSSIBILITY...

ARE YOU SURE YOU HAVE TO LEAVE ALREADY?
YES...WE PROMISED AUNT MIN A VISIT, AND IT'S A TWO-HOUR DRIVE.

SHE BROKE HER HIP, YOU KNOW, AND HASN'T BEEN GETTING AROUND VERY WELL. NOW, IF SHE LISTENED TO HER DOCTOR SHE WOULD BE MUCH BETTER OFF, BUT YOU KNOW AUNT MIN. OF COURSE, THE DOCTORS ALL LOOK LIKE KIDS TODAY, SO WHO CAN BLAME HER? I REMEMBER WHEN I HAD MY HYSTERECTOMY...

COME ON, MOTHER! IT'S LATE!
DADDY'S RIGHT. WE'D BETTER GET GOING IF WE PLAN ON GETTING OUT OF THERE BEFORE DARK,

YOU KNOW HOW AUNT MIN IS... TALK, TALK, TALK...
KIRKMAN & SCOTT

BABY BLUES®

RICK KIRKMAN / JERRY SCOTT

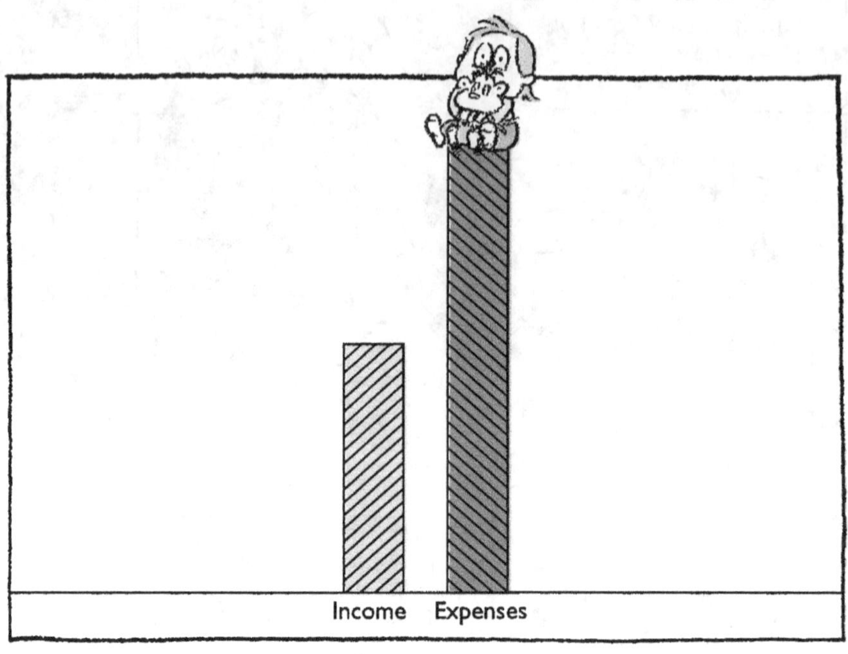

WHACK!
OW!

OH, GREAT.

HEY, WANDA... COME HERE FOR A MINUTE.

WHICH GOES BETTER WITH A BLUE SUIT... THE SESAME STREET BANDAGE OR THE SNOOPY?
GO WITH THE SNOOPY... IT BRINGS OUT THE COLOR IN YOUR EYES.

IS THAT ALL OF THEM?
YEP. THAT'S IT.

YESSS!! I KNEW IT!
WHAT??

YOU DON'T OFFICIALLY HAVE A DIFFICULT CHILD UNTIL YOUR ADVICE BOOKS OUTWEIGH THE KID.
WHICH ONE DID YOU READ THAT IN?

OKAY... ZOE IS WATCHING A VIDEO... HAMMIE IS DOWN FOR A NAP...

IT'S THE PERFECT OPPORTUNITY TO SNEAK OFF AND WRAP A FEW OF THE CHRISTMAS PRESENTS I HAVE SO BRILLIANTLY...

...HIDDEN.
WOOK WHAT WE FOUND!

¿SIGH!¿
WANDA? HONEY? ARE YOU OKAY? WHAT'S WRONG?

IS THERE SOMETHING I CAN DO TO HELP? NAME IT! I'LL DO ANYTHING!
STAY HOME AND TAKE CARE OF THE KIDS WHILE I GO TO WORK, EAT LUNCH IN RESTAURANTS, TALK TO ADULTS, AND WEAR NICE CLOTHES FOR A CHANGE.

OKAY... ALMOST ANYTHING.

THANKS FOR GIVING ME SOME TIME TO MYSELF, DARRYL. I FEEL MUCH BETTER.

I'M SORRY I WAS SUCH A BLUBBERING BASKET CASE EARLIER. THE KIDS JUST HAD ME AT THE END OF MY ROPE.
KIRKMAN & SCOTT

IT'S KIND OF SILLY, NOW THAT I THINK ABOUT IT. IMAGINE! A COUPLE OF SWEET LITTLE KIDS MAKING A GROWN PERSON CRY!

¿SNIFF!¿

DO YOU HAVE TO GO POTTY, ZOE?
YES.

DO YOU NEED ANY HE—
NO! I DON'T NEED HELP! I'M A BIG GIRL! YOU WAIT HERE!

¿SLAM!¿

CAN YOU LIFT ME UP?
KIRKMAN & SCOTT

Baby Blues

BY RICK KIRKMAN / JERRY SCOTT

MOMMY! DADDY! I THINK I TAUGHT HAMMIE A WORD!
REALLY?

OKAY, HAMMIE... SPEAK!
PBBBTH!

IS THAT A WORD?
IS IT A NUMBER?
NO.
NO... ALL YOU'VE TAUGHT HIM TO DO IS TO MAKE AN IMPOLITE SOUND.

YES!

DADDY? I CAN'T GO TO SWEEP!
TRY THE LITTLE TRICK I TAUGHT YOU.

OKAY... ONE... TWO... FWEE...

...I'M STILL AWAKE.
COUNTING SHEEP DOESN'T WORK TOO WELL WHEN YOU ONLY KNOW HOW TO COUNT TO THREE.

LOOK AT US...

...WE'RE A COUPLE OF COLLEGE-EDUCATED, RATIONAL ADULTS, AND YET WE FIND IT NECESSARY TO AVOID OUR OWN CHILDREN.

WHAT DOES THAT SAY ABOUT US AS PARENTS??

THAT WE'RE SMART ENOUGH TO KEEP THE PREMIUM ICE CREAM FOR OURSELVES?
SHH! I THINK THEY FOUND US!
BAM! BAM! BAM!
I SMELL CHOCWIT!

EAT SOME MORE CHICKEN, ZOE.
WHAT?

EAT SOME MORE OF YOUR CHICKEN.
KIRKMAN & SCOTT
WHAT?

YOUR CHICKEN! THE LIGHT BROWN STUFF! PLEASE PUT SOME OF IT ON YOUR FORK, PUT THE FORK IN YOUR MOUTH, THEN CHEW AND SWALLOW!
WHEN?
TAP TAP TAP

WOW! AND ALL MY LIFE I THOUGHT THAT ONLY HAPPENED IN CARTOONS!

WHAT'S THIS SPOT ON THE CARPET?

WHERE?
RIGHT THERE. SEE?

THAT?
YEAH... WHAT IS IT? IT LOOKS WEIRD.

THAT'S THE CLEAN SPOT.
OH. NO WONDER.

YOU'RE NOT CONCERNED THAT HAMMIE ISN'T CRAWLING YET?
NO. THE PEDIATRICIAN SAYS THAT SOME KIDS JUST PREFER TO ROLL.

AREN'T YOU WORRIED THAT HE WON'T LEARN TO WALK FOR A LONG TIME?
NO. MOST ROLLERS JUST SKIP CRAWLING AND GO RIGHT TO WALKING.

THEN NONE OF THIS BOTHERS YOU AT ALL?

BZZZAAP!

WELL, THE STATIC ELECTRICITY HE GENERATES IS SORT OF A DRAWBACK.

DADDY, CAN I AXE YOU A QUESTION?
SURE, ZOE. WHAT'S YOUR QUESTION?

UMM... WHAT DOES IT MEAN?
WHAT DOES WHAT MEAN?

EVERYFING!

WHAT DO YOU THINK?
IT'S EITHER A REALLY GOOD QUESTION, OR A BIG-TIME STALL TACTIC.

BABY BLUES

BY RICK KIRKMAN / JERRY SCOTT

HI, WIDDLE BABY! ARE YOU HUNGWY?

MOMMY HAS YOUR CEWEAL... HEY! DON'T CHEW THAT!
NYUNG NYUNG

STOP GWABBING MY STUFF! GIMME DAT! STOP! YOU'RE DWIVING ME CWAZY!!

PRETTY CUTE, DON'T YOU THINK?
I WAS GOING TO USE THE WORD "FAMILIAR."
GRRRR
KIRKMAN & SCOTT

DID YOU HEAR SOMETHING?
LIKE WHAT?

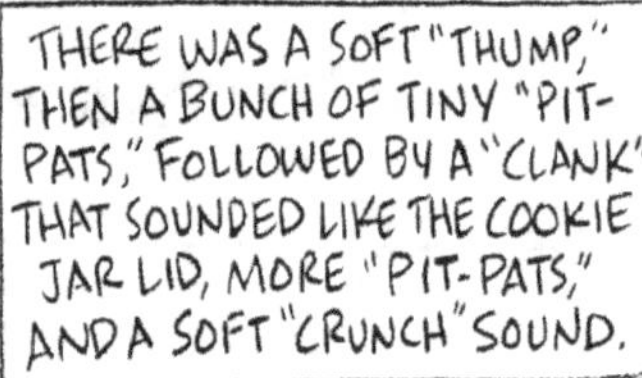

THERE WAS A SOFT "THUMP," THEN A BUNCH OF TINY "PIT-PATS," FOLLOWED BY A "CLANK" THAT SOUNDED LIKE THE COOKIE JAR LID, MORE "PIT-PATS," AND A SOFT "CRUNCH" SOUND.

YOU DIDN'T HEAR THAT...
NO.

I THINK YOU'RE IMAGINING THINGS.
ME TOO. TURN IT UP.
KIRKMAN & SCOTT

EAT YOUR PEAS.
I DON'T WIKE PEAS.

SURE YOU DO! YOU'VE ALWAYS LIKED PEAS! PEAS ARE YOUR FAVORITE VEGETABLE, REMEMBER?
OH YEAH... I FORGOT. I DO WIKE PEAS!

KIRKMAN & SCOTT

I JUST DON'T WIKE THESE PEAS.
YOUR TURN.

IS THERE ANYTHING I CAN DO TO HELP YOU, HONEY?
NO, DEAR, YOU'VE HAD A HARD DAY...

WHY DON'T YOU JUST GO IN THE LIVING ROOM AND PUT YOUR FEET UP WHILE I FINISH THE DISHES, GET THE KIDS READY FOR BED, CLEAN UP THE LIVING ROOM, DO A COUPLE OF LOADS OF LAUNDRY, AND WASH THE CAR.

WELL... OKAY! THANKS!

YOU'D THINK AFTER THIS MANY YEARS OF MARRIAGE, I'D BE ABLE TO RECOGNIZE SARCASM.
KIRKMAN & SCOTT

I WANT DAT! AND DAT! AND DAT! AND DAT, TOO!
THIS IS DISGUSTING!

THESE COMMERCIALS THEY RUN RIGHT BEFORE CHRISTMAS ARE CRIMINAL!

THEY'RE LOUDER, FLASHIER, AND OBVIOUSLY MEANT TO CAPTURE THE ATTENTION OF THE WEAKER, MORE IMPRESSIONABLE MINDS AMONG US!

I'M TURNING IT OFF...
WAIT... I WANT TO SEE THIS... OOH, THAT'S NICE...
KIRKMAN & SCOTT

REMEMBER A COUPLE OF YEARS AGO WHEN OUR CHRISTMAS CARDS WENT OUT LATE, SO WE WROTE "HAPPY HOLIDAYS" INSTEAD OF "MERRY CHRISTMAS" INSIDE?
YEP.

AND THEN THE NEXT YEAR WE WERE EVEN LATER, SO "HAPPY HOLIDAYS" BECAME "SEASON'S GREETINGS"?
HA! YEAH.

KIRKMAN & SCOTT

ANY IDEAS FOR THIS YEAR?
HOW ABOUT "HAPPY EASTER"?

BABY BLUES

RICK KIRKMAN / JERRY SCOTT — BY

IT'S DECEMBER 24th, ZOE!
REALLY?!

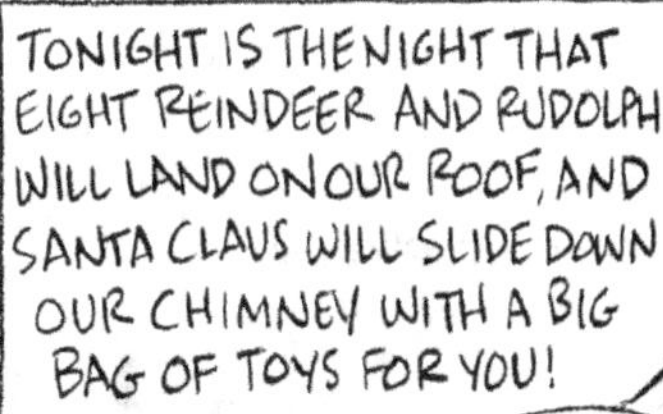

TONIGHT IS THE NIGHT THAT EIGHT REINDEER AND RUDOLPH WILL LAND ON OUR ROOF, AND SANTA CLAUS WILL SLIDE DOWN OUR CHIMNEY WITH A BIG BAG OF TOYS FOR YOU!
WOW!!

TOMORROW MORNING THERE WILL BE LOTS OF PRESENTS AND CANDY UNDER THE CHRISTMAS TREE FOR YOU AND HAMMIE TO OPEN!
YAY!!!

OH BOY! TOYS! OH BOY! TOYS! OH BOY! TOYS!
THE MEDIA SHOULD BE ASHAMED FOR TURNING THIS INTO SUCH A COMMERCIAL HOLIDAY.

CHRISTMAS — 6:00AM

CHRISTMAS — 7:00AM

CHRISTMAS — 7:01AM
IS DAT ALL?

AUNT WONDA! AUNT WONDA!
HI, KIDDO!

MEWWY KWISMUS!
WOW! WELL, MERRY CHRISTMAS TO YOU, TOO, SWEETIE!

SNIFF! LEAVE IT TO A CHILD TO REMIND US WHAT CHRISTMAS IS REALLY ABOUT!

YOU CAN SAY THAT AGAIN.
WHADJA GET ME?

I WISH YOU'D ASKED US BEFORE YOU BOUGHT ZOE A BARBIE DOLL FOR CHRISTMAS, RHONDA.
WHY? WHAT'S WRONG WITH IT?

ZOE'S ONLY TWO-AND-A-HALF YEARS OLD! SHE NEEDS TIME TO BE A KID BEFORE SHE STARTS PLAYING WITH SOME HIGHLY SEXUALIZED, FASHION-DRIVEN SYMBOL OF MATERIALISTIC EXCESS LIKE BARBIE!

OH COME ON! DO YOU HONESTLY THINK A SMART LITTLE KID LIKE ZOE CAN BE AFFECTED BY A SILLY PLASTIC DOLL?

LOOK! BOOBIES!
MAYBE...
KIRKMAN & SCOTT

;SIGH!;

;SIGH!;

DO YOU FEEL OKAY?
I THINK I HAVE POST-HOLIDAY CATALOG WITHDRAWAL.
KIRKMAN & SCOTT

DO YOU THINK IT WAS RIGHT TO TELL ZOE THAT HER BARBIE DOLL IS A HORRIBLE FREAK OF NATURE?
WHY NOT?
AAARGGH! EEK! HELP! HELP!

BARBIE REPRESENTS A WARPED VIEW OF WOMEN! IN ORDER FOR A WOMAN TO HAVE BARBIE'S BODY, SHE WOULD HAVE TO BE OVER SEVEN FEET TALL, WEIGH 120 POUNDS, HAVE A 15-INCH WAIST AND A 47-INCH BUST!!

CAN YOU IMAGINE??
GIVE ME A MINUTE...
KIRKMAN & SCOTT

Baby Blues

by Rick Kirkman / Jerry Scott

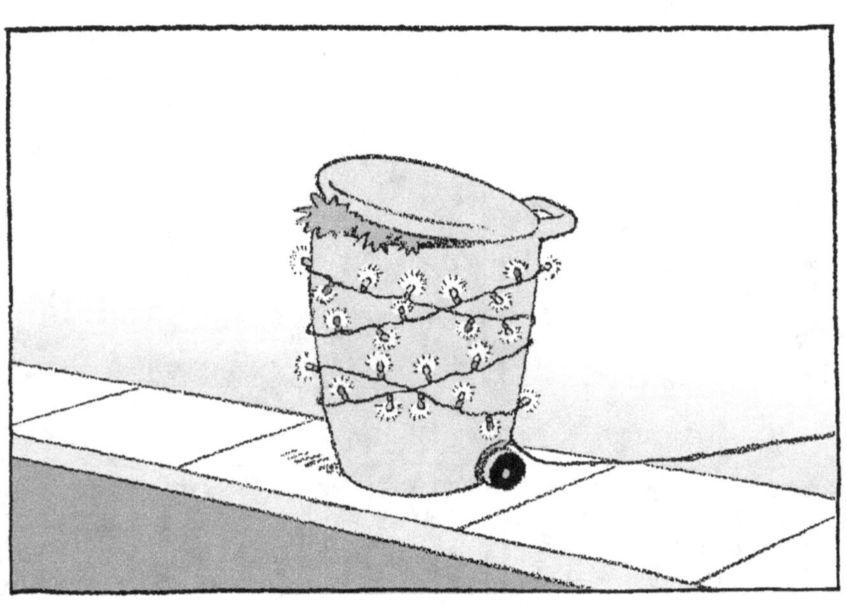

SO, WHERE ARE YOU GUYS GOING FOR NEW YEAR'S EVE?
WE'RE THERE.

YOU MEAN YOU'RE STAYING HOME AGAIN?? DARRYL!
WHAT?? WE LIKE STAYING HOME!

WE DON'T HAVE TO GET DRESSED UP... WE DON'T HAVE TO DRIVE ANYWHERE... WE DON'T HAVE TO SPEND ANY MONEY...

...WE DON'T HAVE TO DANCE... WE DON'T HAVE TO EAT A NICE MEAL... WE DON'T HAVE TO HAVE FUN...
SEE? WANDA AGREES WITH ME!

DO YOU THINK I SHOULD WEAR THIS LONG DRESS OR THE LITTLE BLACK ONE?
THEY'RE BOTH KIND OF DRESSY, AREN'T THEY?

NOT FOR A NEW YEAR'S EVE PARTY... RHONDA SAID IT'S BLACK TIE, REMEMBER?
DO I REALLY HAVE TO WEAR THE TUX?

YES, YOU HAVE TO WEAR THE TUX... AND THE TIE... AND GOOD SHOES... AND THE CUMMERBUND. ANY OTHER QUESTIONS?

DO WE HAVE TO STAY OUT LATE?
MY FIRST CHANCE IN AGES TO GREET BABY NEW YEAR, AND MY DATE IS FATHER TIME.

WE'RE LEAVING NOW. I WANT YOU TO PROMISE ME THAT YOU'LL BE GOOD TONIGHT.

THAT MEANS NO WHINING, NO POUTING, NO COMPLAINING, AND NO TANTRUMS... GOT THAT?
KIRKMAN & SCOTT

AND THAT GOES FOR YOU GUYS, TOO.

WAS THAT A GREAT NEW YEAR'S PARTY, OR WHAT?
OH YEAH.

WHAT A CROWD! WHAT A BAND! WHAT AN EVENING!
PRETTY WILD ALL RIGHT.

WELL. I DON'T KNOW ABOUT YOU, BUT I HAD A BLAST!
I COULD TELL...

ARE YOU SAYING I MADE A FOOL OF MYSELF?
I'M SAYING THAT DOING THE MACARENA TO "AULD LANG SYNE" WAS PUSHING IT.
KIRKMAN & SCOTT

SO TELL ME ABOUT THE NEW YEAR'S PARTY!
OH, YOLANDA! IT WAS SO MUCH FUN!
KIRKMAN & SCOTT

THERE WERE TONS OF PEOPLE, AND THE FOOD WAS GREAT!
HELLO?

HOW ABOUT THE BAND?
THEY WERE UNBELIEVABLE! WE WERE SITTING RIGHT NEXT TO THE SPEAKERS!

DID DARRYL HAVE A GOOD TIME?
YES, BUT I THINK HIS EARS ARE STILL RINGING.
HELLO??

FOR CRYING OUT LOUD... I'LL JUST BURP HIM MYSELF!
NO, WAIT! I'M ALMOST READY!
KIRKMAN & SCOTT

BABY BLUES®
BY
RICK KIRKMAN / JERRY SCOTT

1.
DEAR AUNT RHONDA...
YEAH... DAT'S GOOD.

2.
THANK YOU FOR THE GREAT CHRISTMAS PRESENT.
UH-HUH.

3.
IT IS MY VERY FIRST BARBIE® DOLL, AND I PLAY WITH IT EVERY DAY. LOVE, ZOE

4.
DOES THAT SOUND OKAY?
YEP! BYE!

DID YOU MENTION YOU TOLD ZOE THAT BARBIE® IS A FREAK OF NATURE, NOT THE STANDARD OF BEAUTY?
IS THAT REALLY RELEVANT?
AIEEEEEE
IT'S BARBIE®!! RUN, TEDDY! RUN!!
KIRKMAN & SCOTT

SO, ZOE, WHO DID YOU INVITE TO YOUR BIRTHDAY PARTY?
FWEE FWIENDS... KEESHA, BOGIE AN' BUD.

BUD?? YOU LET HER INVITE BUD??
WHAT'S WRONG WITH BUD?

THAT KID IS A HUMAN WRECKING BALL! A WALKING INSURANCE RATE HIKE! HE'S DESTROYED MORE PERSONAL PROPERTY THAN GUNS & ROSES!

GET SERIOUS... HE PROBABLY JUST DOESN'T GET A LOT OF ATTENTION AT HOME.
THEY SAY HE WAS RAISED BY DACHSHUNDS!
KIRKMAN & SCOTT

I CAN'T BELIEVE YOU LET ZOE INVITE BUD TO HER BIRTHDAY PARTY!
WHY?

THIS IS BUD WE'RE TALKING ABOUT! BUD THE DISMANTLER!
GIVE IT A BREAK.

DING-DONG!
I'M TELLING YOU, THIS KID IS TROUBLE.
JUST ANSWER THE DOOR.
KIRKMAN & SCOTT

HAPPY BIRFDAY.
I REST MY CASE!

HOW'S IT GOING IN THERE?
PRETTY WELL.
PRETZELS

WE NEED MORE PUNCH, MORE PRETZELS—

HERE YOU GO, ZOE'S DAD.

OH, AND CALL A PLUMBER.
BUD!!!
KIRKMAN & SCOTT

OKAY, KIDS... LET'S ALL SING!

HAPPY BIRTHDAY TO YOU...
JINGLE BELLS! JINGLE BELLS!
THE WHEELS ON THE BUS GO 'ROUND AND 'ROUND!
LONDON BRIDGE IS FAWWING DOWN...
ITSY-BITSY SPIDER...

ACTUALLY, I MEANT THAT WE SHOULD ALL SING THE SAME SONG...
NOW CAN WE BLOW UP THE CANDLES?
EASY, BUD...
KIRKMAN & SCOTT

WELL, OUR LITTLE GIRL IS THREE YEARS OLD.
YEP. HARD TO BELIEVE, ISN'T IT?

IT SEEMS LIKE JUST YESTERDAY THAT SHE WAS A TINY BABY... HELPLESS AND UNAWARE OF THE WORLD AROUND HER.
THINGS SURE CHANGE, DON'T THEY?

ZOE, WILL YOU BRING ME THAT PLATE AND CUP OVER THERE?
KIRKMAN & SCOTT

OF COURSE, THE MORE THEY CHANGE, THE MORE THEY STAY THE SAME...
ZOE?...ZOE?... HELLO-O-O-O-O!

OPEN UP! OPEN! OPEN!

ZOE, HOW CAN I BRUSH YOUR TEETH IF YOU WON'T OPEN YOUR MOUTH? COME ON! OPEN UP!
¡SNICKER!¡

I'M SORRY...YOU SHOULD HEAR... IT JUST SOUNDED...

GREAT. IF YOU THINK IT'S SO FUNNY, YOU TRY.
KIRKMAN & SCOTT

Baby Blues

...AN' I WANNA SLIDE DOWN DA HILL, AN' MAKE A SNOWMAN, AN' FROW SNOWBALLS, AN' DO SNOW ANGELS, AN'...
OKAY! OKAY! JUST LET ME FINISH DRESSING HAMMIE!

FINALLY!
YAY!

CLICK!

I'M DONE!

HERE, HAMMIE... WANT A BITE?
NO, ZOE!

HAMMIE ISN'T QUITE READY FOR SOLID FOOD, SWEETHEART.

BESIDES, LITTLE BABIES ONLY EAT FOOD THAT HAS BEEN MASHED.
OH....

HERE, ZOE... LET DADDY HELP YOU WITH THAT MILK.
I CAN DO IT MYSELF!

BUT IT'S REALLY FULL, AND I—
IT'S MINE!

OKAY! IT'S YOURS! JUST LET ME GIVE YOU A H—
STOP!

NOW LOOK WHAT YOU DID!

MAY I HELP YOU?
Are you prepared?

HUH?
Someday soon, the world as we know it will be gone and everything will be different.

PROMISES... PROMISES...

QUICK! HELP ME PICK UP THE HOUSE! WE ONLY HAVE FIFTEEN MINUTES!
YIPES!

OKAY... I'LL PICK UP THE TOYS, YOU GET THE BATHROOMS, I'LL DUST AND VACUUM, AND WE'LL BOTH DO THE KITCHEN!
GOOD PLAN!

BY THE WAY... WHO'S COMING OVER?
NOBODY...

...I JUST FIND THAT THE HOUSE GETS CLEANED BETTER WHEN WE'RE IN A PANIC.

ZOE! LOOK!
HAMMIE GOTS A TOOTH!

HAMMIE GOTS A TOO-OTH! A TOO-OTH! HAMMIE GOTS A TOO-OTH!

CHOMP!
EEEEE-EEEE!

WHAT'S WRONG?
HAMMIE GOTS A TOOTH.

BABY BLUES®

BY RICK KIRKMAN / JERRY SCOTT

I INVITED THE BREWERS OVER FOR DINNER ON WEDNESDAY.
THE BREWERS? THE PEOPLE WITH THAT PROBLEM WHERE THEY CAN'T HAVE KIDS?

THE TERM IS INFERTILITY. AND, YES, THAT'S THEM.

BUT CAN'T YOU FIND A BETTER WAY TO REFER TO THEM THAN IN TERMS OF WHETHER OR NOT THEY HAVE CHILDREN?
YEAH... SURE... LET'S SEE...

HOW ABOUT, "THE COUPLE THAT GETS A FULL NIGHT'S SLEEP?" OR, "THE COUPLE WITH DISPOSABLE INCOME?" OR, "THE COUPLE WITH DECENT FURNITURE?"...

I THINK IT'S GREAT THAT WE'RE HAVING THE BREWERS OVER FOR DINNER, BUT WHAT ARE WE GOING TO TALK ABOUT?
WHAT DO YOU MEAN?

EVER SINCE YOU TOLD ME THAT THEY ARE HAVING FERTILITY PROBLEMS, I DON'T KNOW WHAT TO SAY TO THEM.
OH, COME ON!

YOU SAY THE SAME THINGS YOU WOULD TO PEOPLE WHO HAVE KIDS...

...EXCEPT YOU CAN SPEAK FASTER AND USE BIGGER WORDS.
WHAT? I DIDN'T GET THAT...
HEE HEE HEE HEE!

LOOK, YOU TWO DON'T HAVE TO AVOID TALKING ABOUT YOUR KIDS JUST BECAUSE WE CAN'T HAVE CHILDREN.
THAT'S RIGHT. INFERTILITY ISN'T A DISEASE.

WE MAY NEVER BE ABLE TO HAVE KIDS OF OUR OWN, BUT THAT DOESN'T MEAN WE LOVE CHILDREN ANY LESS.
WOW. THAT'S AN AMAZING ATTITUDE.
YEAH. SO MATURE.

FOR WHAT IT'S WORTH, I THINK YOU TWO WOULD MAKE GREAT PARENTS.
IN FACT, YOU MAY BE OVERQUALIFIED.

GOOD NIGHT! THANKS FOR COMING OVER!
THE BREWERS ARE REALLY NICE PEOPLE.

ALL THIS TIME I ASSUMED THAT JUST BECAUSE THEY DIDN'T HAVE KIDS THAT THEY WERE SELFISH YUPPIE SCUM—
WHEN, IN FACT, THEY'RE A SWEET COUPLE WITH FERTILITY PROBLEMS.

I SURE LEARNED A LESSON TONIGHT.
DON'T JUDGE A BOOK BY ITS COVER?
SELFISH YUPPIE SCUM IS AN ENDANGERED SPECIES.
CLICK!

TODAY'S PROGRAM WAS BROUGHT TO YOU BY THE TWELFTH LETTER IN THE ALPHABET AND THE SQUARE ROOT OF SIXTEEN.

PBS

"L" AND "4."
PBS

I'M TOO DUMB FOR "SESAME STREET"!

SERIOUSLY, WHEN DO YOU THINK WE SHOULD START WEANING HAMMIE?

I DON'T KNOW... A LOT OF PEDIATRICIANS ARE SAYING THAT INFANTS SHOULD BE BREAST-FED FOR AT LEAST A YEAR.
A YEAR??

SIX MORE MONTHS?...

WELL, I DON'T THINK PEDIATRICIANS WOULD RECOMMEND IT UNLESS THEY HAD GOOD REASONS.
I DON'T THINK PEDIATRICIANS SHOULD RECOMMEND IT UNLESS THEY HAVE BREASTS!

BABY BLUES

RICK KIRKMAN / JERRY SCOTT BY

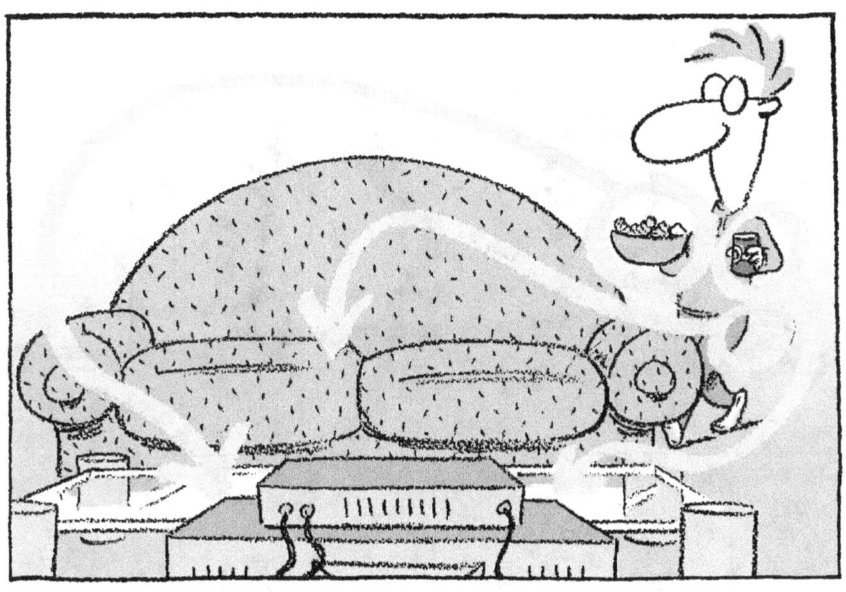

SO HOW WAS YOUR DAY?
NOT BAD... BUT THE KIDS WERE ACTING UP IN THE GROCERY STORE.

IT WAS SO WEIRD! ONE MINUTE I HAD A COUPLE OF UNRULY MONSTERS, AND THE NEXT MINUTE I HAD THE SWEETEST, MOST WELL-BEHAVED KIDS IN THE STORE!

WOW! HOW DID YOU ACCOMPLISH THAT?

I ACCIDENTALLY STARTED PUSHING SOMEONE ELSE'S CART.

DADDY, CAN I HAVE A COOKIE?
I DON'T KNOW... IT'S PRETTY CLOSE TO DINNERTIME. GO ASK MOMMY.

MOMMY?
YES, SWEETIE?

SHE SAID, "YES, SWEETIE."
OH. OKAY.

SLAM!

SLAM!

SLAM!

WHEN YOU THINK ABOUT IT, WE'VE WASTED A LOT OF MONEY ON DRESSERS AND HANGERS.

IZ YOU MOMMY'S WIDDLE POOKUMS? HMMM?

WELL, YETZ YOU IZ! YETZ YOU IZ! BOOKA-BOOKA-BOOKA!
KIRKMAN & SCOTT

WHEN THEY TAWK LIKE THAT, IT MEANS THEY'RE HAPPY.

WHAT DOES HAMMIE HAVE IN HIS HANDS?

SIGH! TRUCKS. HE FOUND THEM IN ZOE'S ROOM THIS MORNING AND HE HASN'T LET GO OF THEM SINCE.

I DON'T THINK HE EVEN PUT THEM DOWN WHILE I FED HIM.
OH... GOOD.
KIRKMAN & SCOTT

THEN THAT EXPLAINS THE TIRE TRACKS ACROSS YOUR CHEST.

TELL DADDY WHAT YOU DID TODAY, ZOE.

WELL FIRST WE PWAYED CIRCLE AN' WE WENT AROUND—MOMMY WIKES APPLE JUICE TOO!—I SAID, "I HAVE AN IDEA!", AN' SO—KNOW WHAT? BIRDS FWY WA-A-A-Y UP HIGH INNA SKY AN' THEN 'CUZ WATCHES KNOW WHAT TIME IT IS.
KIRKMAN & SCOTT

DID YOU GET ALL THAT?
I THINK SHE HAS A 200-MEGAHERTZ MIND WITH A 10-MEGAHERTZ MOUTH.

BABY BLUES

BY RICK KIRKMAN / JERRY SCOTT

HACK! SNORT! SNIFF!
COUGH! WHEEZE! GROAN!

COUGH! COUGH! SNIFF!
HEY, TOM! YOU DON'T SOUND SO GOOD.
I KNOW.

DO YOU HAVE A COLD?... FLU?... BRONCHITIS?... OR WHAT?
I HAVE A THREE-YEAR-OLD IN PRESCHOOL.

EWWWW... ALL OF THE ABOVE, THEN, HUH?

WAA-AAA-AA!
TEETHING PAIN?
YEAH...POOR LITTLE GUY!

LET'S TRY SOME OF THIS.
TOPICAL ANALGESIC FOR THE RELIEF OF PAIN CAUSED BY TEETHING.

CHOMP!
AAAAGH!

WHAT DO YOU KNOW... IT WORKS!

SMILE, HAMMIE! SHOW DADDY YOUR NEW TOOTH!

THAT'S IT! GOOD! LET ME GET A LITTLE BIT CLOSER NOW...

HOLD IT...HOLD IT... NOW FOCUS, AND...

OH GREAT— NOW SOMETHING'S WRONG WITH THE CAMERA!

SO HAMMIE ROLLS INSTEAD OF CRAWLING? THAT'S SO CUTE!
YOU REALLY THINK SO?

YOU DON'T THINK IT'S WEIRD OR TROUBLING OR ALARMING?
NO! I JUST THINK HE'S FOUND A WAY TO GET AROUND THAT WORKS FOR HIM!

BLESS YOU!!

...NOT THAT CRITICISM BOTHERS ME...
OF COURSE NOT.
KIRKMAN & SCOTT

EEEEK! IT'S A MONSTER! QUICK! HIDE!

HANG ON! I'M COMING!!

HYAHH! OOF! SMACK!

PWETEND I'M FAWWING OFF A CWIFF AND YOU DIE SAVING ME.
WE MAY BE WATCHING TOO MANY ANIMATED ADVENTURES AROUND HERE.

I CAN'T BELIEVE THAT HAMMIE ALREADY HAS A TOOTH... DID ZOE GET HER FIRST TOOTH THIS EARLY?
YES. ALMOST EXACTLY THE SAME AGE.

YEAH... I GUESS IT WAS AT SIX MONTHS, BUT IT SEEMED LIKE LONGER.

SIX MONTHS USED TO SEEM LIKE SIX MONTHS... NOW SIX MONTHS SEEMS LIKE SIX WEEKS!

SO IS TIME SPEEDING UP, OR AM I SLOWING DOWN?
DO YOU REALLY WANT TO KNOW?

WHATTER YOU DOING, MOMMY?
PUTTING ON MY MAKEUP.

WHY?
SO I'LL LOOK PRETTY.

BUT YOU'RE ALWEDDY PWETTY!

WANNA HEAR A GOOD WAY TO GET A COOKIE?

BABY BLUES®
BY
RICK KIRKMAN / JERRY SCOTT

MY FIRST GOLF BAG
MY FIRST DOCTOR KIT

I'M THE DOCTOR AN' YOU'RE THE SICK PERSON, OKAY, DADDY?
OKAY DOC.

OOOOOHHH!
AAARGH! I NEED A DOCTOR!
OKAY JUSTA MINUTE.

FIRST, I TAKE YOUR TEMPERATURE...
OW!
JAB

...THEN I LOOK IN YOUR EARS...
HEY!

NOW WHERE'S MY OTHER STUFF?
BOOF!

SAY AAAAHH...
AADCCCK!

GOTTA GO... AMB'LANCE IS COMING!
AAGH! OOOCH! OWW!

WHAT'S WRONG WITH YOU?
I NEED A NEW HEALTH PLAN.
KIRKMAN & SCOTT

ZOE MADE DARRYL THE CUTEST VALENTINE'S CARD...
LET ME SEE.

SHE GLUED ON THE SEQUINS AND PIPE CLEANERS AND PAINTED IT ALL BY HERSELF.
HOW SWEET!

"Roses are red,
Violets are sad.
Take Mommy to dinner.
She needs it real bad."
KIRKMAN & SCOTT

I HELPED WITH THE WORDING.
YOU CAN'T REALLY TELL.

;AHEM!;

OOOH! CANDY AND FLOWERS! HOW SWEET!
AND THAT'S NOT ALL...

TA-DAAAH!
;GASP!; OH, DARRYL! JUST WHAT I WANTED...
KIRKMAN & SCOTT

...A REAL BABY-SITTER!
IT'S JUST A RENTAL... GO GET DRESSED.
HAPPY VALENTINE'S DAY, MRS. MacPHERSON.

I'M REALLY GETTING SICK OF COMMUTING.

I WONDER WHAT IT WOULD BE LIKE TO HAVE A JOB WHERE I COULD BE MY OWN BOSS AND JUST WORK AT HOME...?

OH.
KIRKMAN & SCOTT

VVVV VVVV VVVV VV-SKNXXTTT!

VVVVV VVVVV VV-KKX XXVREE EEEEP!

VVVVVVVV VV-XXXXK KPPPHII P-P-P-P-P!!

EVIL PEOPLE SHOULD BE REINCARNATED AS VACUUM CLEANERS IN HOMES WITH CHILDREN.

THWACK!

TRIP! Thunk! SCRAPE!

BONK!

I THINK WE'D BETTER POSTPONE ZOE'S CHECKUP.
YEAH...SHE LOOKS TOO MUCH LIKE SHE NEEDS TO SEE A DOCTOR TO GO SEE THE DOCTOR.

DADDY?
YES, SWEETHEART?

DO YOU... UM...DO YOU... UMMM... DO YOU... UMMM...
DO I WHAT?

DO YOU... UMM...DO YOU... UMMM... DO YOU... UMMM...DO YOU... UMMM... DO YOU...UM... DO YOU... UMMM...
ZOE, IF YOU CAN'T ASK ME THE QUESTION, I CAN'T GIVE YOU AN ANSWER.

WELL...DOES DADDY WANT TEA OR WATER WITH DINNER?
HE CAN'T GIVE ME AN ANSWER.

BABY BLUES

BABY BLUES ®
BY
RICK KIRKMAN / JERRY SCOTT

HA! HA! THAT'S THE TIME THAT WE TRIED TO PAINT THE LIVING ROOM WHEN YOU WERE JUST A YEAR OLD!
HOW 'BOUT DAT ONE?
AWWW...YOUR FIRST GLASS OF CHERRY KOOL-AID...
AND SEE THIS? THAT WAS THE TIME YOU "HELPED" DADDY CHANGE THE OIL IN THE CAR...REMEMBER?
UH-UH.
PURPLE!
THAT'S RIGHT! THAT'S FROM THE DAY YOU DECIDED TO PAINT DADDY A PICTURE WITH GRAPE JELLY.
WAIT, YOU GUYS! I WANT TO SEE SOME OF THESE, TOO!
SO WHERE ARE THE PICTURES?
WHAT PICTURES? WE'RE LOOKING AT THE STAINS ON YOUR SWEATPANTS.
KIRKMAN & SCOTT

WHAT ARE YOU DOING?
RELAX. IT'S JUST A TINY BIT OF MASHED POTATO... I WANT TO SEE WHAT HAMMIE WILL DO.

HEY! HE ATE IT! DID YOU SEE THAT, ZOE?

THE FIRST TIME I GAVE YOU A BITE OF SOLID FOOD YOU SPIT IT RIGHT BACK OUT AT—
KIRKMAN & SCOTT

—ME.

THIS IS A TEST. FOR THE NEXT TEN SECONDS WE'LL BE TESTING THIS CHILD'S EMERGENCY DISTRESS SIGNAL. THIS IS ONLY A TEST.

BATH TIME.

NOOOOOOOOOOOOOOOOOOOOOOOOOOOOOOOOO!

THIS HAS BEEN A TEST.
MY GLASSWARE!
KIRKMAN & SCOTT

HI THERE, ZOE!

IT'S ALMOST TIME FOR DINNER, SO GO WASH YOUR HANDS, SWEETIE!
AND DON'T FORGET TO USE SOAP!

BYE FOR NOW!

I STILL THINK THERE'S SOMETHING VERY WRONG WITH THIS...
HEY, YOU WANTED TO GET HER ATTENTION, RIGHT?
KIRKMAN & SCOTT

I'M DONE!
WAIT! AREN'T YOU GOING TO FINISH YOUR LUNCH?

YOU LEFT THREE-FOURTHS OF YOUR HOTDOG, MOST OF YOUR POTATO SALAD, AND DIDN'T EVEN TOUCH YOUR GREEN BEANS!
YOU CAN HAVE IT.

PAT PAT

THAT'S THE TROUBLE WITH LEFTOVERS... THEY EITHER GO TO WASTE, OR GO TO WAIST.
KIRKMAN & SCOTT

LOOK AT THAT! I'LL BET IT WON'T BE LONG UNTIL HAMMIE STARTS PULLING HIMSELF UP ON THINGS.

YEAH...WE'D BETTER PUT ALL OF OUR VALUABLE OR IRREPLACEABLE STUFF UP OUT OF HIS REACH.

KIRKMAN & SCOTT

WELL... THAT WAS EASY!
IF NOT DEPRESSING.

I GOTS A QUEXTION.
YOU MEAN, "I HAVE A QUESTION."

I HAVE A QUEXTION.

QUESTION. Kweś·chən.
QUEXTION.

OKAY, NEVER MIND... WE'LL WORK ON THAT LATER. WHAT'S YOUR QUESTION?

HOW DO YOU SAY "QUEXTION"?
KIRKMAN & SCOTT

Baby Blues

BY RICK KIRKMAN / JERRY SCOTT

MONDAY
SOMETIMES I THINK...

TUESDAY
...OUR LIVES HAVE...

WEDNESDAY
...BECOME SOMEWHAT...

THURSDAY
...PREDICTABLE.
I KNEW YOU WERE GOING TO SAY THAT.

BLUE! THIRTY-TWO! BLUE! THIRTY-TWO! HUT! HUT! HUT!
THIP!
YES!
KIRKMAN & SCOTT

I CAUGHT IT!
SO THAT'S WHAT HAPPENS TO ALL THE DOUBLE-SIDED TAPE...

OH MY GOSH!

WHAT'S WRONG?

HAMMIE HAS GROWN OUT OF THE LITTLE PINK BUNNY SHIRT THAT MY MOM GAVE HIM.

DARN!
THANK GOODNESS!
KIRKMAN & SCOTT

DO YOU WANT MOMMY TO PUT YOUR HAIR IN A PONYTAIL OR PIGTAILS TODAY?
PIGTAILS!

OKAY... PIGTAILS IT IS!
NO! PONYTAIL!

FINE.
NO! PIGTAILS! NO! PONYTAIL! NO! PIGTAILS! NO! PONYTAIL! NO! PIGTAILS! NO! PONYTAIL!

THAT'S WEIRD... I JUST FOUND THE ENTIRE "LETTING TODDLERS MAKE CHOICES" CHAPTER FROM THE BABY BOOK WADDED UP IN THE TRASH.
HI!!

PARENTS OF ONE CHILD
AWWWW...
SIGH!
Z
OFTEN PUT CHILD TO BED, THEN STARE AT CHILD FOR LONG PERIODS OF TIME.

PARENTS OF TWO CHILDREN
LONG TIME NO SEE.
Z
YOU LOOK FAMILIAR...
Z
OFTEN PUT CHILD TO BED, THEN STARE AT EACHOTHER.

HA! HA! DID YOU SEE THAT?
HE'S SO CUTE... I WISH WE WOULD'VE GOTTEN THAT ON TAPE!
PBBBBTH!

PBBBBTH!

ZOE! THAT'S NOT POLITE!
DISGUSTING! GO WIPE OFF YOUR FACE!

BABY BLUES

BY RICK KIRKMAN / JERRY SCOTT

WHAT'S DAT?
PAT PAT

IT'S A CLOTH DIAPER... SEE? I PUT IT ON MY SHOULDER WHEN I'M BURPING HAMMIE.

THAT WAY, IF HE SPITS UP, IT WON'T GET ALL OVER MY—
BLORP!

—SHIRT.
DIDN'T WORK.

IT'S MORNINGTIME, DADDY! GET UP!

LET'S PWAY! LET'S EAT BWEAKFAST! LET'S WATCH TV! LET'S PAINT!

—ZIP!
KIRKMAN & SCOTT

DON'T YOU WISH YOU HAD THAT MUCH ENERGY FIRST THING IN THE MORNING?
IT'S MORNING??

LET'S SEE THAT FIRST TOOTH OF YOURS, BIG FELLA!

COME ON... OPEN UP! OPEN! OPEN!

I KNOW HOW YOU CAN MAKE HIM OPEN HIS MOUTH... DO WHAT MOMMY DOES!
WHAT'S THAT?

SHOW HIM YOUR NIPPLE.
KIRKMAN & SCOTT

YOU KNOW WHAT'S SO GREAT ABOUT KIDS? THEIR INNOCENCE.

THE PURE HONESTY AND SWEETNESS, UNSPOILED BY THE VULGARITIES OF THE OUTSIDE WORLD.

SEEYA, BUTTHEAD.
KIRKMAN & SCOTT

WELL, UNSPOILED BY MOST OF THE VULGARITIES OF THE OUTSIDE WORLD.
WHERE DID YOU HEAR THAT WORD???

WHAT ARE YOU THINKING ABOUT?

THE KIDS, TAXES, EDUCATION. BIRTHDAY PARTIES, TONIGHT'S DINNER, TOMORROW NIGHT'S DINNER. NEXT THANKSGIVING. CHRISTMAS. GRAY HAIR. HEALTH INSURANCE. MY CLOTHES. LOSING WEIGHT. NEW FURNITURE. AND THE FUDGE BROWNIES I MADE FOR DESSERT.

WHAT ARE YOU THINKING ABOUT?
THE FUDGE BROWNIES.
KIRKMAN & SCOTT

SHOW MOMMY YOUR PRETTY NEW TOOTH, HAMMIE!

COME ON! SMILE! SMILE! SMILE!
FLASH!
YOU FINALLY GOT A PICTURE OF THE TOOTH? HOW DID IT COME OUT?
GREAT!

I GOT THE PICTURE I WANTED, PLUS AN IDEA FOR NEXT HALLOWEEN'S JACK-O'-LANTERN.
KIRKMAN & SCOTT

BABY BLUES®

by RICK KIRKMAN / JERRY SCOTT

I HAFTA GO POTTY!

OKAY... DO YOU NEED ME TO HELP YOU GET UNDRESSED?
NO.

DO YOU WANT ME TO HELP YOU GET DRESSED AFTERWARDS?
DO YOU WANT ME TO GO WITH YOU?
NO.
NO.
DO YOU WANT ME TO WAIT OUTSIDE THE DOOR?
NO.

THEN WHAT DO YOU WANT ME TO DO??
CLAP WHEN I'M DONE.
KIRKMAN & SCOTT

KNOCK IT OFF, ZOE! SOMETIMES YOU ACT JUST LIKE YOUR MOTHER!

...WHICH IS A VERY NICE THING! YESSIREE! GOOD GIRL!
PAT! PAT!

OH! HI, DEAR!

WHAT DOES "CRETIN" MEAN?
IT'S JUST YOUR MOMMY'S WAY OF SAYING THANKS.
KIRKMAN & SCOTT

...AND BOTH KIDS HAVE EAR INFECTIONS, THE ANTIBIOTICS WENT UP $10, SOMEBODY DENTED THE CAR DOOR IN THE PARKING LOT, THE WASHING MACHINE SOUNDS FUNNY AGAIN, AND HAMMIE GOT STUCK UNDER THE COUCH.

WOW!

REMEMBER WHEN I WOULD CALL YOU TO ASK WHAT WAS NEW AND YOU'D SAY "NOTHING"?
BARELY.
KIRKMAN & SCOTT

MOMMY! DADDY! I'M GONNA PUT ON A SHOW FOR YOU.
THAT'S GREAT!
HOW NICE!

UH...UMMM... WELLLL...

I'LL BE WIGHT BACK!

THE ITSY-BITSY SPIDER CRAWLED UP THE WATER SPOUT...
SHE'S SHY... ISN'T THAT CUTE?
FOR ME, IT RUINS THE VISUAL IMPACT OF THE PERFORMANCE.
KIRKMAN & SCOTT

I HAFTA GO POTTY!

I JUST WENT POTTY!
KIRKMAN & SCOTT

I'M PWAYING WIF MY DOLLS! I'M BEING A BIG GIRL! I HAVE BLUE EYES! I WIKE 'ASGHETTI!

NOW I'M JUST STANDING HERE YELLING FOR NO REASON!
DO YOU EVER CATCH YOURSELF SORT OF LOOKING FORWARD TO THE "EMPTY NEST SYNDROME"?

DADDY! I CAN'T SLEEP!
TRY COUNTING SHEEP!

I'M AFWAID OF SHEEP! ORANGE KITTENS?
THEN COUNT KITTENS!
SURE! FINE! COUNT ORANGE KITTENS!

WAAAAAAAAAA!
NOW WHAT'S WRONG?
KIRKMAN & SCOTT

I DON'T WIKE ORANGE KITTENS!
AAAGGGHH!

BABY BLUES®

RICK KIRKMAN / BY JERRY SCOTT

WHERE WOULD I FIND THE MEASURING SPOONS?
PROBABLY THE SAME PLACE YOU'D FIND ALL THE OTHER KITCHEN UTENSILS.

OH YEAH. WHAT WAS I THINKING?

DO YOU NEED ANYTHING WHILE I'M OUT HERE?

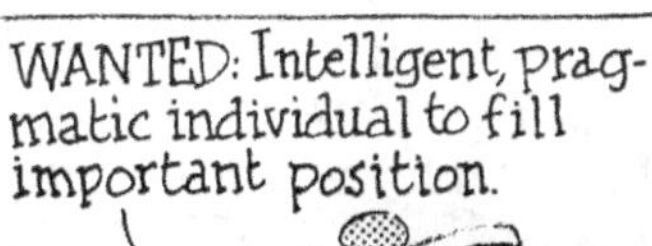

Applicant should be experienced, enthusiastic, creative, and able to handle difficult management decisions. Compensation negotiable. Transportation provided. References required.

HI, WHAT CAN I DO FOR YOU?
I'M HERE TO INTERVIEW FOR THE BABY-SITTING JOB.

OH...HA!HA! THERE MUST BE SOME MISTAKE... WE WERE LOOKING FOR SOMEONE A LITTLE MORE EXP—
I HAVE SIX BROTHERS AND SISTERS, I'VE BEEN CHANGING DIAPERS SINCE I WAS THREE, AND I'LL WORK FOR TWO BUCKS AN HOUR.

WELL, THAT'S VERY IMPRESSIVE, BUT I...
PLUS, I CAN FIX COMPUTERS.

HONEY, THERE'S SOMEONE I'D LIKE YOU TO MEET...
KIRKMAN & SCOTT

EXCUSE US, KIKI... WE'LL BE RIGHT BACK.
OKAY.

YOU CAN'T BE SERIOUS! SHE'S SO YOUNG!
I KNOW, BUT SHE SEEMS LIKE SHE'D BE A REALLY GOOD BABY SITTER! LET'S GIVE HER A—

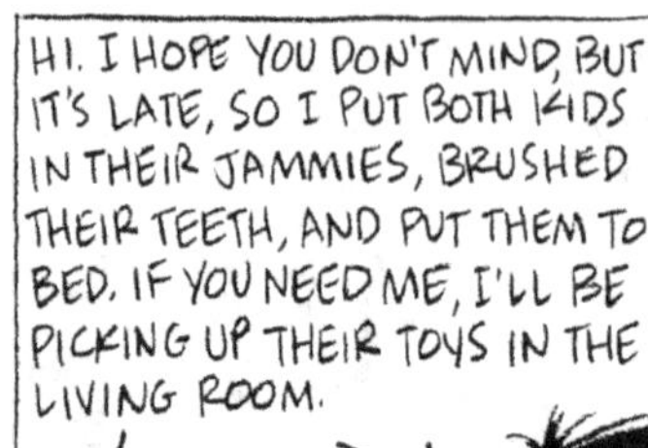

HI. I HOPE YOU DON'T MIND, BUT IT'S LATE, SO I PUT BOTH KIDS IN THEIR JAMMIES, BRUSHED THEIR TEETH, AND PUT THEM TO BED. IF YOU NEED ME, I'LL BE PICKING UP THEIR TOYS IN THE LIVING ROOM.
KIRKMAN & SCOTT

—CHANCE.
GIVE HER A CHANCE?? LET'S ADOPT HER!

I THINK YOU ARE A VERY PRETTY GIRL!
FROZEN FOOD

WHAT DO YOU SAY TO THE LADY, ZOE?

I THINK YOU HAVE A REALLY FAT BOTTOM.

YOU KNOW HOW I SAID YOU SHOULD ALWAYS TELL THE TRUTH? WELL, I'VE CHANGED MY MIND.
KIRKMAN & SCOTT

BABY BLUES

BY RICK KIRKMAN / JERRY SCOTT

...FIVE... SIX... SEVEN... EIGHT... NINE... TEN! WEADY OR NOT, HERE I COME!

DADDY? DADDY?

DADDYYYY!
I'M RIGHT HERE, ZOE! IT'S OKAY!

YOU'RE KIND OF NEW TO THIS GAME, AREN'T YOU?
YOU PLAY WITH ME, MOMMY... HE'S TOO EASY.
KIRKMAN & SCOTT

THAT'S A PACIFIER. THEY'RE FOR BABIES.
UH-HUH.
THUP! THUP! THUP!

HAMMIE IS A BABY, SO HE HAS A PACIFIER. I'M NOT A BABY. I'M A BIG GIRL. I DON'T HAVE A PACIFIER ANYMORE. PACIFIERS ARE FOR BABIES.
RIGHT.

THUP! THUP! THUP! THUP!

WAAAA·AAAA·AA!
BABY!
KIRKMAN & SCOTT

BOYS ARE DOCTORS AN' GIRLS ARE CHEERLEADERS.
WHAT?? NO! NO! NO! NO! NO!

GIRLS CAN BE DOCTORS, TOO, ZOE! THEY CAN ALSO BE LAWYERS, PHARMACISTS, TEACHERS, FIREFIGHTERS, ARTISTS, WRITERS, POLICE OFFICERS...

GIRLS CAN BE WHATEVER THEY WANT!
WHAT CAN BOYS BE?

USUALLY WHATEVER GIRLS WANT THEM TO BE.
DON'T COMPLICATE THIS, OKAY?
KIRKMAN & SCOTT

WHY ARE YOU CHANGING HAMMIE'S DIAPER?
THAT'S A SILLY QUESTION... BECAUSE HE'S A BABY AND HE STILL WETS HIMSELF!

NO... I MEAN, WHY ARE YOU CHANGING HIM AN' NOT DADDY?

CAN SOMEBODY TELL ME WHY I SUDDENLY HAVE A MOIST NAKED BABY IN MY LAP?
KIRKMAN & SCOTT

I SAID COME HERE SO I CAN BRUSH YOUR HAIR!
NOOO!

JUST HOLD STILL!
STOP TWISTING!
NO!
OWW! LEMME GO!

THERE! I GUESS THAT'LL HAVE TO DO.
WAAAA!

YOU MISSED A SPOT.
KIRKMAN & SCOTT

HA! HA! HA! LOOK AT THIS PICTURE OF ME WHEN I WAS PREGNANT WITH HAMMIE!
PHOTOS

WHAT A TUBB-O! WHAT A HEIFER! MOOOOOOOO!
PHOTOS

PHOTOS

THIS IS WHERE I SAY SOMETHING LIKE, "DON'T BE SILLY, DEAR. YOU'RE BEAUTIFUL WHEN YOU'RE PREGNANT." RIGHT?
YOU'RE CATCHING ON.
KIRKMAN & SCOTT
PHOTOS

Baby Blues

by Rick Kirkman / Jerry Scott

KNOCK! KNOCK!
WHO'S THERE?
BLAPGM.
BLAPGM WHO?

BLAPGM PBBTH! PBBBTH! HA! HA! HA! HA! HA!
REAL FUNNY. NOW I HAVE ONE.

KNOCK! KNOCK!
OLIVE.
WHO'S THERE?
OLIVE WHO?
I LOVE YOU!

KIRKMAN & SCOTT
I DON'T GET IT.

WHAT ARE YOU EATING?
NOTHIN'.

GASP! CREME EGGS! THE EXPENSIVE ONES, TOO!
GET AWAY! THEY'RE MINE!

YOU PUT STALE JELLYBEANS IN MY EASTER BASKET WHILE YOU WERE HIDING THESE FOR YOURSELF?? OF ALL THE...
I CAN EXPLAIN! I CAN EXPLAIN!

OKAY... EXPLAIN.
I THOUGHT I COULD GET AWAY WITH IT.
KIRKMAN & SCOTT

PLEEZE?
NO, ZOE.

PLEEZE? PLEEZE? PLEEZE?
NO!

PLEEEEEEZE?
ZOE, I SAID "NO." WHAT DO YOU THINK IT MEANS WHEN YOUR DADDY SAYS "NO"?

GO ASK MOMMY?
KIRKMAN & SCOTT

DO YOU REALIZE THAT WE'RE GOING TO HAVE TWO KIDS IN COLLEGE AT THE SAME TIME?
YUP.

HOW ARE WE GOING TO DO IT? HOW WILL WE AFFORD IT?
EASY...

...YOU PUT AWAY A LITTLE MONEY EACH MONTH WHILE THE KIDS ARE GROWING UP, AND WHEN THEY'RE READY FOR COLLEGE...

...YOU PANIC.
THANKS. I FEEL MUCH BETTER NOW.
KIRKMAN & SCOTT

LOOK! HAMMIE IS WALKING!

GRUNT! LOOK! HAMMIE IS FLYING!

LOOK! HAMMIE IS READING!
ABC

CHOMP!
WAAAAAA!
LOOK! HAMMIE IS DEFENDING HIMSELF!
ABC

WHAK!
OW!

THONK!
OUUCH!

GOTCHA!
OOOOF!
THUD!
KIRKMAN & SCOTT

TIME FOR BED... DADDY'S TIRED.
BLESS YOU.

BABY BLUES®

BY
RICK KIRKMAN / JERRY SCOTT

!
ICE

ZOE! THESE TOYS OF YOURS ARE STILL IN THE MIDDLE OF THE LIVING ROOM FLOOR!

COME AND PICK THIS STUFF UP RIGHT NOW!

I MEAN IT! DO YOU HEAR ME??
OKAY! I'M COMING!

THAT'S MORE LIKE IT! YOU'RE A BIG GIRL NOW, AND YOU'RE OLD ENOUGH TO LISTEN TO MOMMY.

I SHOULDN'T HAVE TO SCREAM AT YOU MORE THAN ONCE.
KIRKMAN & SCOTT

CAN I HELP YOU FIX SOMETHING, DADDY?
HUH? UH... OKAY, SURE!

HERE YOU GO... HAVE A WRENCH.

I DON'T THINK YOU CAN DO MUCH DAMAGE WITH—

—THAT.
WHAT ELSE CAN I FIX?
KIRKMAN & SCOTT

WHEN I GWOW UP, I'M GONNA BE A FIREFIGHTER!
THAT'S GREAT, ZOE!

AN' A DOCTOR!
AN' A BALLERINA!
TERRIFIC!
WONDERFUL!

ARE YOU IMPRESSED?
I'M TRYING TO PICTURE WHAT SHE'S GOING TO WEAR TO WORK.
KIRKMAN & SCOTT

HEY!
WHAT?

IT'S 6 A.M. AND I DON'T REMEMBER GETTING UP ONCE WITH THE KIDS LAST NIGHT!

DO YOU REALIZE WHAT THIS MEANS??
I SURE DO!

IT MEANS IT'S YOUR TURN TONIGHT!
KIRKMAN & SCOTT

SLAM!

I THINK I'LL GO CLEAN THE GUTTERS, HOSE DOWN THE DRIVE-WAY, AND WASH THE CARS.
WOW! THAT'S PRETTY AMBITIOUS!

IT'S EITHER THAT OR MATCH UP A DRYERFUL OF BABY SOCKS.
HEY! WAIT A MINUTE!
KIRKMAN & SCOTT

ON SECOND THOUGHT, MAYBE HAMMIE COULD SKIP HIS NAP TODAY...
WIMP.
KIRKMAN & SCOTT

RING!

HELLO? HELLO?
RING!
KIRKMAN & SCOTT

HELLO? HELLO? HELLOOOO!!!
RING! RING!

YOU HAVE TO PICK IT UP FIRST.
OH.
RING!

Baby Blues

by Rick Kirkman / Jerry Scott

BUNNY CALLED.
WHAT DID SHE WANT?

SOMETHING ABOUT WANTING TO GIVE YOU AN ARTICLE ON HOW TO MAKE FESTIVE WREATHS OUT OF OLD ORANGE JUICE CANS, CEREAL BOXES AND EGG SHELLS.

JUST STAY OUT OF OUR GARBAGE CAN, OKAY??

TO SOME PEOPLE RECYCLING IS NOT JUST A DUTY... IT'S AN OBSESSION.

I THINK ZOE IS GETTING BORED WITH STAYING HOME ALL DAY.
WHAT SHOULD WE DO... GIVE HER A SET OF KEYS TO THE CAR?
=SIGH=

NO, I THINK WE SHOULD PUT HER IN PRESCHOOL FOR A COUPLE OF MORNINGS A WEEK.
YOU DO??

YES! SHE WOULD BE OUT AMONG OTHER PEOPLE, LEARNING NEW STUFF... JUST THINK OF ALL THE THINGS SHE COULD PICK UP OUT THERE!
FORGET IT.

WHY??
BECAUSE OF ALL THE THINGS SHE COULD PICK UP OUT THERE!

ZOE, HOW WOULD YOU LIKE TO GO TO PRESCHOOL?
LET ME TRY.
NO.

GUESS WHAT, ZOE?... YOU GET TO GO TO PRESCHOOL!
I'VE GOT IT... I'VE GOT IT...
NO!

IF YOU'RE REALLY, REALLY GOOD, MOMMY AND DADDY WILL LET YOU GO TO PRESCHOOL!
NO!
=SIGH=

WELL, IT WOULD HAVE BEEN PRETTY EXPENSIVE ANYWAY...
I WANNA GO! I WANNA GO!

DARRYL! GUESS WHAT?... I FOUND THE PERFECT PRESCHOOL FOR ZOE.

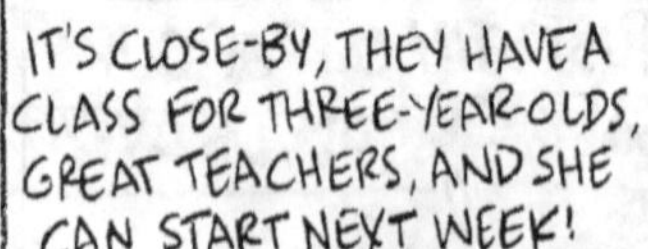

IT'S CLOSE-BY, THEY HAVE A CLASS FOR THREE-YEAR-OLDS, GREAT TEACHERS, AND SHE CAN START NEXT WEEK!

THERE'S ONLY ONE PROBLEM. IT'S THE BEST PRESCHOOL IN THE CITY, AND THEY THINK ZOE HAS THE PERFECT QUALIFICATIONS.
SO WHAT'S THE PROBLEM?

THEY'RE NOT SURE WE DO.
KIRKMAN & SCOTT

MR. AND MRS. MacPHERSON, I'M GEOFFREY ENGLE, THE HEADMASTER HERE AT REDFIELD PRESCHOOL.

REDFIELD IS THE FINEST PRE-SCHOOL IN THE STATE, WINNER OF THE PRESTIGIOUS "EDUCA-TOR'S TROPHY" THREE YEARS RUNNING, AND THIS YEAR'S RECIPIENT OF THE COVETED "PLATINUM CRAYON AWARD."
MY!
WOW!

NOW, HOW MAY I HELP YOU?
WE'D LIKE TO ENROLL OUR DAUGHTER HERE.

WONDERFUL! WHEN WILL SHE BE BORN?
I SMELL WAITING LIST.
KIRKMAN & SCOTT

WELL, WE FOUND A REALLY GOOD PRESCHOOL FOR ZOE TODAY.
HEY, THAT'S GREAT!
MY SCHOOL!

SHE STARTS NEXT WEEK: TUESDAYS AND THURSDAYS, NINE TO ELEVEN-THIRTY.
TERRIFIC!
SCHOOL! SCHOOL! SCHOOL!

GREAT!
WONDERFUL!
EXCITING!
A MILESTONE!
YOU BET!
YESSIREE!

WAAAAAA!
KIRKMAN & SCOTT

Baby Blues

RICK KIRKMAN / JERRY SCOTT

IT'S THREE O'CLOCK IN THE MORNING, ZOE...WHAT'S THE MATTER??
DERE'S SOMETHING SCARY UNDER MY BED!

HE'S REALLY UNDER THERE! LOOK!
WOULD YOU MIND?
OKAY...SURE. WHAT THE HECK. I'LL TAKE A—

AIEEEEEE!

MONSTER??
HUMONGOUS DUST BUNNY.
SEE?
KIRKMAN & SCOTT

I MADE AN APPOINTMENT FOR ZOE TO HAVE HER HAIR CUT BEFORE SHE GOES TO PRESCHOOL.
REALLY? AT THE BEAUTY SHOP!

YEAH. IT'LL BE FUN. WE CAN TAKE SOME "BEFORE" AND "AFTER" PICTURES.

OF HER, ORUS?
KIRKMAN & SCOTT

THIS IS A BEAUTY SHOP, ZOE.
WAAAAA!

AND THIS IS RACHELA...SHE'S GOING TO CUT YOUR HAIR.
WAAAAAA!

YOU GET TO SIT IN THIS BIG CHAIR THAT GOES UP AND DOWN IN FRONT OF A BIG MIRROR!
KIRKMAN & SCOTT

AND WHEN YOU'RE FINISHED, THERE WILL BE A TREAT!
WAAAAA!
FOR HER, OR ME?

WAAAAAAAAAAAAA! WAAAAAAAAA! WAAAAAAAAAAAAAAAAAAAAA! WAAAAAAAAAAA!
HOW WOULD YOU LIKE ME TO CUT IT?
YES! THAT SOUNDS FINE!

HOW SHORT SHOULD IT BE?
YES, SHE JUST TURNED THREE.

JUST TELL ME THE STYLE!
OKAY, LET'S ALL SMILE!

AREN'T YOU GOING TO ASK ME HOW I WANT IT CUT?
: SIGH :
KIRKMAN & SCOTT

ALL FINISHED! WHAT DO YOU THINK?
IT'S CUTE! IT'S ADORABLE! IT'S HER!
SNIF!

THANKS AGAIN! BYE!
Salon

IS SHE STILL LOOKING?
NOPE, SHE'S GONE.

COMB! BRUSH! COMB! BRUSH!
KIRKMAN & SCOTT

ZOE, I WANT YOU TO—

SHHH! QUIET, DADDY! MY BABY IS SLEEPING!
BUT... I...

LOOK WHAT YOU DID! YOU WOKE HER UP! OH DEAR! THAT DOES IT!

I THOUGHT YOU WERE GOING TO MAKE ZOE PICK UP HER TOYS...
IT'S A LONG STORY...
KIRKMAN & SCOTT

BABY BLUES

RICK KIRKMAN / JERRY SCOTT BY

AAAAAGH!

RING?
RING!

HI, HONEY, HOW'S IT GOING?
HA!

IF YOU HAD ANY IDEA HOW I SPEND MOST OF MY TIME DURING THE DAY, YOU'D FALL DOWN ON YOUR KNEES IN GRATITUDE EVERY TIME YOU SAW ME!
YOU JUST HAD TO RE-ROLL THE TOILET PAPER AGAIN, RIGHT?
KIRKMAN & SCOTT

OUR LITTLE GIRL'S FIRST DAY OF PRESCHOOL...
ARE YOU EXCITED?
ARE YOU READY?
ARE YOU AFRAID?
NO.
NO.
YES.

ACTUALLY, I WAS TALKING TO ZOE.
CAN WE GO NOW?
KIRKMAN & SCOTT

HAPPY HANDS PRESCHOOL
SPRING SING
KIRKMAN & SCOTT

NOW THAT ZOE IS OFFICIALLY IN PRESCHOOL, I HAVE TO FIGURE OUT WHAT TO DO WITH MY MORNINGS.

IF I ADD THE TIME IT TAKES ME TO DRIVE HOME AND BACK, AND THE TIME IT TAKES ME TO GET HAMMIE IN AND OUT OF THE CAR SEAT...

...AND I SUBTRACT THAT FROM THE HOURS ZOE IS IN SCHOOL, IT LEAVES ME EXACTLY....

...NOTHING.
HAPPY HAND PRESCHOOL
SCREECH!
KIRKMAN & SCOTT

Baby Blues

by Rick Kirkman / Jerry Scott

BONK!

HI, ZOE! HOW WAS YOUR FIRST DAY OF PRESCHOOL?
GREAT. THIS IS TRENT. HE'S MY NEW FRIEND.

WELL, HI THERE, TRENT. IT'S NICE TO MEET YOU! WHAT CUTE FRECKLES YOU HAVE.
POP!
POP!
POP!
POP!

POP!
POP!
POP!
POP!
POP!
POP!
POP!
POP!
POP!
POP!
POP!

THEY ARE FRECKLES, AREN'T THEY, TRENT?
CHICKEN-POX!!!
POP!
POP!
POP!
POP!
POP!

I CAN'T BELIEVE THAT ZOE WAS EXPOSED TO CHICKENPOX ON HER VERY FIRST DAY OF PRESCHOOL!
WHAT'S CHIPPEN POPS?
MEDICAL DICT...

CHICKEN-POX. IT'S A DISEASE THAT KIDS GET.
WHAT'S A DIZEEZE?
MEDICAL DICT...

A DISEASE IS A SICKNESS. YOU MIGHT GET SICK IN A WEEK OR SO BECAUSE YOU PLAYED WITH TRENT.
OH.

PLAYING WITH BOYS WILL MAKE ME SICK?
YES, REMEMBER THAT.
YOU'RE NOT HELPING HERE!
KIRKMAN & SCOTT

NO, ZOE. THE ANSWER IS NO.

OKAY, MOMMY.

ALL RIGHT... WHAT'S THE CATCH?
KIRKMAN & SCOTT

ARE YOU GUYS PLAYING CATCH?
HUH?

CATCH: WHEN YOU THROW THE BALL TO EACH OTHER AND YOU CATCH IT, IT'S CALLED "CATCH."

BONK!
KIRKMAN & SCOTT

THEN THAT'S NOT WHAT WE'RE PLAYING.

DO YOU EVER WONDER IF WE'RE PROVIDING THE KIDS WITH A GOOD CHILDHOOD?

LET'S SEE... THEIR OWN ROOMS, GOBS OF TOYS, STACKS OF BOOKS AND VIDEOS, ACCESS TO A COLOR TV AND A VCR, A PRIVATE BATHROOM, RECREATIONAL ACTIVITIES, A CAR AND DRIVER TO TAKE THEM ANYWHERE THEY NEED TO GO...

THIS ISN'T CHILDHOOD... IT'S A RESORT!
KIRKMAN & SCOTT

THAT OUGHT TO DO IT, HAM.
HAM? NO. THIS IS DAIRY... THE MEAT COUNTER IS DOWN THERE.

NO... HE'S HAM. THAT'S HIS NAME!
NAMING A CHILD AFTER A PORK PRODUCT... TALK ABOUT WEIRDOS.

HAM IS SHORT FOR HAMISH! GET IT? HAM? HAM?

THIS IS THE DAIRY CASE... THE MEAT COUNTER IS DOWN THERE.
SIGH!
KIRKMAN & SCOTT

Baby Blues

by Rick Kirkman / Jerry Scott

YOLANDA? IT'S WANDA.

I DON'T THINK YOU WANT KEESHA TO COME OVER TODAY... ZOE HAS CHICKENPOX.

KNOCK! KNOCK! KNOCK!
HANG ON... SOMEBODY IS AT THE DOOR.

YOLANDA...
COUGH UP SOME GERMS! WE WANT TO GET IT OVER WITH.

THAT MAKES ALMOST EVERY MOTHER IN THE NEIGHBORHOOD WHO HAS BROUGHT HER KID TO BE EXPOSED TO ZOE'S CHICKENPOX.
ALMOST?

YEAH, EVERY ONE BUT BUNNY, NEXT DOOR.
OH, OF COURSE! A CASE OF CHICKENPOX MIGHT UPSET HER PERFECT LIFE!

OKAY, ZOE... SNEEZE!

HI, HONEY... HOW ARE THE KIDS DOING?
JUST PEACHY.

THEIR CHICKENPOX IS ITCHING LIKE CRAZY, THEY'RE BORED, AND THE VCR JUST STOPPED WORKING.
POOR LITTLE KIDS...

IS THERE ANYTHING THAT I CAN PICK UP ON THE WAY HOME THAT WOULD HELP?

A QUART OF RUM AND TWO TICKETS TO HAWAII.
I MEANT FOR THE KIDS.

HI.
HI.

IT'S PRETTY QUIET...THINGS MUST HAVE CALMED DOWN SINCE I CALLED YOU EARLIER.
YEAH... FOR A WHILE, ANYWAY.

I FINALLY GOT THEM INTERESTED IN SOMETHING THEY COULD DO TOGETHER.
REALLY? LET'S GO SEE.

ALL DONE!
CONNECT THE CHICKEN-POX??
OKAY, YOU THINK OF SOMETHING!

YOU'RE REALLY PROUD OF YOUR KIDS, AREN'T YOU, DARRYL?
I SURE AM. THEY'RE AMAZING.

IT'S SO REWARDING TO WATCH THEM GROW UP. I CAN'T WAIT TO SEE THEM BECOME STRONG, INDEPENDENT PEOPLE OUT ON THEIR OWN!

YEAH. I FEEL THE SAME WAY ABOUT MY KIDS.
THAT'S NICE.

HOW OLD ARE YOURS?
TWENTY-EIGHT AND THIRTY-TWO.

1. Drive Zoe to preschool
2. Pick up Zoe from preschool
3. Buy Groceries
4. Drop off stuff
5. Pick up stuff
6. Take kids here
7. Take kids there
THIS MAKES NO SENSE.

WHAT?

WHY AM I CALLED A STAY-AT-HOME MOM WHEN THE ONE THING I NEVER DO IS STAY AT HOME?

BABY BLUES®

BY RICK KIRKMAN / JERRY SCOTT

...I READ SOMEWHERE THAT IF YOU FASTEN THE BRACKET—
DADDY! DADDY! DADDY!

ZOE, DADDY IS ON THE PHONE! IT'S NOT POLITE TO INTERRUPT.
OH.

ANYWAY, IF YOU FASTEN THE BRACKET TO THE —
DADDY! DADDY! DADDY!

WHAT DOES "INTERRUPT" MEAN?
KIRKMAN & SCOTT

WAKE UP, ZOE! HURRY! WE HAVE TO GET READY FOR PRESCHOOL!
ZZZZ.

EAT! GIVE ME YOUR FOOT! POINT YOUR TOES! CHEW! SWALLOW!

TUCK YOUR SHIRT IN! DON'T RUN! BE CAREFUL! HAVE FUN! I LOVE YOU!
KIRKMAN & SCOTT

I USED TO THINK I WAS BUSY... THEN I BECAME THE MOTHER OF A PRESCHOOLER!
ROOKIE, EH?

I'M THE DOCTOR AN' YOU BE THE SICK GUY.
OKAY.

SAY "AHH."
AHHHHHHH...

AHHHHHH—
ZOE! HOW MANY TIMES HAVE I TOLD YOU TO STOP TAKING THAT FILTHY STICK OUT OF THE TRASH??

AHHHHHHHHHH...
KIRKMAN & SCOTT

HANG ON! I'M COMING TO RESCUE YOU!

GRUNT! OOF! ERF! AARRGH!

AACK! UNFF! MMMAARGH!

I DON'T THINK HAMMIE WANTS TO BE RESCUED RIGHT THIS MINUTE, ZOE.
TOO BAD.
KIRKMAN & SCOTT

I WAS THINKING ABOUT SOMETHING IMPORTANT TODAY.

WHAT WAS IT?
I DON'T REMEMBER.

WELL, WAS IT ABOUT MONEY?
I DON'T KNOW.
THE KIDS?
BEATS ME.
US? OUR PARENTS?
I HAVE NO IDEA.
KIRKMAN & SCOTT

YOU STAY HOME RAISING KIDS FOR THREE YEARS AND WE'LL SEE HOW GOOD YOUR MEMORY IS!

GNAW! GNAW! GNAW! GNAW!
DO YOU HEAR SOMETHING?
YEAH.

GNAW! GNAW! GNAW! GNAW!
IT SOUNDS LIKE CHEWING OR SOMETHING.
YOU DON'T SUPPOSE IT'S TERMITES, DO YOU?

GNAW! GNAW! GNAW! GNAW!
I DON'T KNOW... I'M NOT SURE WHERE IT'S—

—COMING FROM.
HEY! HAMMIE HAS ANOTHER TOOTH!
KIRKMAN & SCOTT

BABY BLUES

BY RICK KIRKMAN / JERRY SCOTT

MOMMY!
HI, ZOE!

HOW WAS PRESCHOOL TODAY?
I DUNNO.

WELL, WHAT DID YOU DO?
I DUNNO.
DID YOU HEAR STORIES?
I DUNNO.
DID YOU DRAW PICTURES?
I DUNNO.
DID YOU PLAY ON THE SLIDE?
I DUNNO.

PRESCHOOL CAUSES AMNESIA.

BOOGERNOSE!
ZOE!

WE DON'T USE LANGUAGE LIKE THAT AROUND HERE.
OH.

I WANT YOU TO TELL HAMMIE YOU'RE SORRY, AND PROMISE ME YOU'LL NEVER USE THAT WORD AGAIN.
I'M SORRY, I PROMISE.

HONESTLY! I DON'T KNOW WHERE SHE PICKS UP ALL THAT STUFF!
HIYA, BOOGERNOSE!

BPTH MNGL.
HAMMIE WANTS HIS TEDDY BEAR.
OKAY...

ONGL NFIG.
HAMMIE SAYS HE WOULD LIKE THAT TRUCK, TOO.
WOW! YOU REALLY UNDERSTAND HIM?

MMPTH GMM MAA!
HAMMIE SAYS HE WANTS HIS PACIFIER.
A TRANSLATOR! THIS IS GREAT!

MERPP.
AN' HE THINKS YOU SHOULD GIVE ME FIVE COOKIES.
NICE TRY.

BEFORE CHILDREN...
YEAH.
HOW CAN PEOPLE LET THEIR KIDS GO OUT DRESSED LIKE THAT?

AFTER CHILDREN...
YEAH.
WELL, AT LEAST SHE'S COVERED...
KIRKMAN & SCOTT

HOLD IT RIGHT THERE!

I JUST FINISHED CLEANING THE LIVING ROOM.

I DON'T EVER WANT TO HAVE TO CLEAN UP THE KIND OF MESS THAT WAS IN HERE AGAIN. UNDERSTAND?
YES.

HI, ZOE, WHAT'S NEW?
MOMMY SAID FROM NOW ON YOU HAVE TO CLEAN THE LIVING ROOM.
KIRKMAN & SCOTT

WELL IT'S ONE FOR THE MONEY, TWO FOR THE SHOW... THREE TO GET READY, NOW GO, CAT, GO!

DON'T YOU STEP ON MY BLUE SUEDE SHOES!

I USED TO SING THAT TO YOU ALL THE TIME WHEN YOU WERE A BABY.
OH.
KIRKMAN & SCOTT

WERE YOU MAD AT ME?

BABY BLUES®
BY
RICK KIRKMAN / JERRY SCOTT

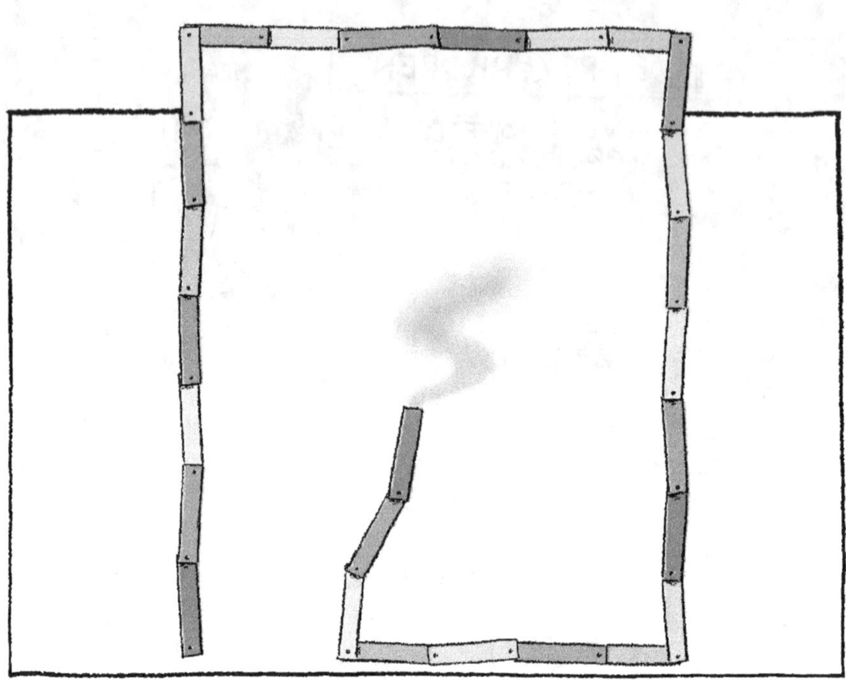

WHAT ARE THOSE THINGS THE KIDS ARE PLAYING WITH, BUNNY?
OH! YOU HAVEN'T SEEN THOSE?

IT'S A BRAND-NEW TOY CONCEPT FROM SWITZERLAND... EVERYBODY HAS THEM!
THEY DO?
CLICK! CLICK!

SURE! SEE? THEY'RE TOTALLY NON-VIOLENT, EDUCATIONAL, EARTH-FRIENDLY, UNISEX TOYS DESIGNED TO PROMOTE COOPERATIVE PLAY AMONG CHILDREN.
YOU'RE THE ONLY PERSON I KNOW WHO HASN'T HEARD ABOUT THEM!
I AM?

WOULD YOU LIKE TO SEE THE BROCHURE?
OKAY... SURE... I GUESS SO... THAT WOULD BE GREAT.

CLICK!
CLICK!

POW! BANG-BANG! GOTCHA!
POW! POW! POW! POW! AAAAAGH!
NEVER MIND!
KIRKMAN B SCOTT

IT WAS REALLY GREAT TO SEE YOU, NANCY!
SAME HERE! WE SHOULD GET TOGETHER ONE OF THESE WEEKENDS.

GOOD IDEA... I'LL CALL YOU.

BUT RIGHT NOW I HAVE TO GO,.. HAMMIE IS GETTING REALLY HUNGRY.
REALLY! HOW CAN YOU TELL?

SUBTLE HINTS.
KIRKMAN & SCOTT

MY DOLLY!

WAAAAAAAAA! THAT'S NO FAIR!

HAMMIE GAVE YOUR DOLL BACK, ZOE... WHAT'S NOT FAIR ABOUT THAT?
SNIF!

HE LEFT BEFORE I COULD HIT HIM.
KIRKMAN & SCOTT

UNNH!
MMFFT!
AARRGH!
OOF!
KIRKMAN & SCOTT

ONE!
ZOE IS LEARNING TO PUT HER SOCKS ON BY HERSELF!
DO YOU THINK IT'S WORTH IT?

WANDA! DO WE HAVE ANY MORE DIAPERS?
I THINK THERE'S A PACKAGE IN THE LINEN CLOSET!

COULD YOU—
I CAN'T GET THEM FOR YOU NOW... I'M BUSY!

WELL, HOW CAN I— HE MIGHT—WHAT IF HE—

KIRKMAN & SCOTT

PBBTH!

PBBTH! PBBTH! PBBTH!

PPPBBBBBTH!

KIRKMAN & SCOTT

ATTENTION! EVERYBODY BE QUIET!

NO TALKING! NO SCREAMING! NO CRYING! AND NO PLAYING THE DRUMS!

'CUZ MY DADDY IS SLEEPING!
KIRKMAN & SCOTT

BABY BLUES

BY RICK KIRKMAN / JERRY SCOTT

POW! POW! GOTCHA!

ZOE, WHAT WERE YOU JUST DOING?
SHOOTIN' A GUN.

WHERE DID YOU LEARN ABOUT GUNS?
TOBY TAUGHT ME AT SCHOOL! BANG! BANG!

:SIGH!:
I GUESS THERE'S MORE TO EDUCATION THAN WHAT YOU GET FROM A TEACHER...
AND, HE KNOWS LOTS OF FUNNY NAMES FOR OUR BODY PARTS!

BRAAAP!
SAY "EXCUSE ME," ZOE.

WHY?
BECAUSE YOU JUST DID SOMETHING IMPOLITE. WHEN YOU DO SOMETHING IMPOLITE, YOU SHOULD SAY "EXCUSE ME."

EVERY TIME?
EVERY TIME.

S'CUSE ME. S'CUSE ME. S'CUSE ME. S'CUSE ME. S'CUSE ME.
OR YOU COULD TRY NOT TO DO IT AT ALL!

YESTERDAY WAS THE FIRST OF JUNE, ZOE, CAN YOU SAY "JUNE"?
JOOON.

JUNE RHYMES WITH MOON. AND SPOON, AND BALLOON!

THAT'S FUN TO SAY, ISN'T IT? JUNE... MOON... SPOON... BALLOON...

BABOON... LOON... CARTOON... SPITTOON...
JUST HOW MANY MISTER ROGERS SHOWS HAS MOMMY BEEN WATCHING?
A LOT.

WAAAA AAAAA!
NOW YOU SIT THERE FOR TWO MINUTES AND THINK ABOUT CHANGING YOUR BEHAVIOR, YOUNG LADY!

WAAAAAAAA!

WAAAAAAA!
WHY ONLY TWO MINUTES?
THAT'S ALL I CAN STAND.

SHRIEK! HA! HA! HA! HA! HA!

HA! HA! HA! HA! HA! HA!
WHAT IN THE WORLD IS SO FUNNY?

GIGGLE! GASP! DADDY GIGGLE! IS WEARING SNORT! CLOWN PANTIES!!! HA! HA! HA! HA!

AND YOU WONDER WHY I LIKE BRIEFS BETTER THAN BOXERS...
SHRIEK! SEE???

LOOK, MOMMY AN' DADDY! I DRESSED MYSELF!

OH!
YOU SURE DID!

IS THAT WHAT YOU WANT TO WEAR TO SCHOOL?
UH-HUH.

WHAT DO YOU THINK?
I DON'T KNOW WHETHER TO HURT HER PRIDE OR SWALLOW MINE.
I LOOK GOOD!

BABY BLUES

BY RICK KIRKMAN / JERRY SCOTT

Riiing!

H'LO? WHO IS IT, PLEASE?

OH, HI AUNT RHONDA! GOOD... GOOD... UH-HUH... UH-HUH... UH-HUH... YES...

IS YOUR MOMMY THERE?
JUST ABOUT.
YOU'RE ≥PANT!≤ SUPPOSED TO ≥WHEEZE!≤ GIVE ME A HEAD START ≥GASP!≤ REMEMBER?

SO, ZOE, WHAT DID YOU DO AT PRESCHOOL TODAY?
WELL, WE ALL SAT IN OUR PLACES AND LISTENED, THEN WE WENT HOME.

AND WHAT ELSE?
NOTHIN'.

WHAT'S WRONG? DOESN'T THAT SOUND LIKE A FUN DAY?
IT SOUNDS LIKE MY DAY.

≥GIGGLE!≤
≥GIGGLE!≤
WHAT'S SO FUNNY?

≥CHUCKLE!≤ BUNNY IS ALL WEIRDED OUT BECAUSE BOGART IS PRETENDING THAT ALL OF HIS TOYS ARE GUNS!

≥SNORT!≤ I SHOULDN'T LAUGH, BUT IT'S JUST SO HILARIOUS!

DON'T YOU SEE THE IRONY?
ALMOST...
STICK 'EM UP!

DADDY, I'LL BE THE BEAUTI- FUL PRINCESS AND YOU BE THE HANDSOME PRINCE.
OKAY.

HAMMIE WILL BE THE GOOD KING, THIS DOLL WILL BE THE QUEEN, AN' THESE GUYS WILL BE DOROTHY, TOTO AN' THE MUNCHKINS.
KIRKMAN & SCOTT

WHAT ABOUT MOMMY?
YEAH! WHAT WILL I BE?
SAME AS USUAL.

WHY DO I ALWAYS HAVE TO BE THE WICKED WITCH?
'CUZ YOU'RE GOOD AT IT.
THAT WAS A COMPLI- MENT, RIGHT, ZOE?

SO HAMMIE DOESN'T WANT TO TAKE NAPS ANYMORE, HUH?
NOPE, THIS IS DEFINITELY A NEW PHASE HE'S IN.

WELL, HAVE YOU TRIED—
YOU NAME IT, I'VE TRIED IT.

WELL, IT'S HARD TO BELIEVE NOTHING WORKS.
TRUST ME ON THIS.
KIRKMAN & SCOTT

DING- DONG!
KIKI IS HERE!!

HI, KIKI. HOW ARE Y—
OKAY, MOMMY AN' DADDY. GO NOW... BYE!

HAMMIE IS ASLEEP... EMER- GENCY NUMBERS ARE BY THE PHONE... SNACKS ARE IN THE FR—
HAVE A GOOD TIME!
GO! GO! GO!
KIRKMAN & SCOTT

IS IT POSSIBLE FOR A BABYSITTER TO BE TOO GOOD AT HER JOB?
I WISH YOU LIVED HERE INSTEAD OF MOMMY AN' DADDY.

Baby Blues

BY RICK KIRKMAN / JERRY SCOTT

MOMMY, CAN HAMMIE AN' ME HAVE SOME ICE CREAM?
ZOE, YOU KNOW BETTER THAN THAT.

HAMMIE IS JUST A BABY. HE CAN'T EAT ICE CREAM.
OH YEAH...

KIRKMAN & SCOTT
HMMM...

OKAY, THEN I'LL EAT HIS FOR HIM.
HEY! THAT'S MY TRICK!

RAWWRRRR!

THAT'S BRYAN. HE'S A DINOSAUR.
RRRRRR...
KIRKMAN & SCOTT

WHAT KIND OF DINOSAUR IS HE?
I THINK HE'S A PLANT-EATER TODAY.

WHEN HE'S A T-REX, I PLAY INSIDE.
SNAP!

BRYAN, THIS IS MY MOMMY. MOMMY, THIS IS BRYAN. HE'S A DINOSAUR.
NICE TO MEET YOU, BRYAN.

RAWWWR!

DOES HE ALWAYS ROAR AT PEOPLE LIKE THAT?
NO...
STOMP! STOMP!

...ONLY WHEN HE'S GOING TO BITE.
KIRKMAN & SCOTT

ARE YOU SAYING THAT BRYAN PRETENDS HE'S A DINOSAUR EVERY DAY??
ᴇSIGH!ᴇ YES, I'M AFRAID SO.
STOMP! STOMP! STOMP!

IT ISN'T JUST A THING HE DOES DURING RECESS?
NO... HE'S PRETTY MUCH A FULL-TIME DINOSAUR.
RAWWRR!

HE DOESN'T ACT LIKE THIS IN CLASS, DOES HE?
OF COURSE NOT! WE HAVE RULES ABOUT BEHAVIOR...
KIRKMAN & SCOTT

WELL, THAT'S GOOD TO—
...HE'S NOT ALLOWED TO EAT ANY CHILDREN OR LAY EGGS UNTIL AFTER STORY TIME.
CHOMP! CHOMP!
AIEEEEE!

DID YOU KNOW THAT THERE'S A KID IN ZOE'S PRESCHOOL WHO CONSTANTLY PRETENDS HE'S A DINOSAUR?
HOW WEIRD!

I'M GLAD YOU THINK SO! THE TEACHER DOESN'T SEEM TO THINK IT'S STRANGE AT ALL!
ARE YOU KIDDING? OF COURSE IT'S STRANGE!

YOU'RE NOT GOING TO SEE OUR SON WALKING AROUND PRETENDING TO BE SOME PREHISTORIC MONSTER!
GOOD!

HE'S GOING TO PRETEND HE'S AN AIRPLANE, LIKE A NORMAL KID... RIGHT, HAMMIE?
KIRKMAN & SCOTT

DARRYL, HAMMIE HAS A DOCTOR'S APPOINTMENT THIS MORNING... COULD YOU TAKE ZOE TO PRESCHOOL?
UH... WELL...

GEE, I PROMISED STAN I'D GET IN EARLY TO FINISH UP OUR REPORT BEFORE THAT REALLY IMPORTANT MEETING AT TEN... AND I HAVE A CONFERENCE CALL AT NINE, SO...

SO YOUR ANSWER IS...?
SURE, I'D BE GLAD TO.

NEVER TRY TO IMPRESS A MOTHER OF TWO WITH YOUR BUSY SCHEDULE.
KIRKMAN & SCOTT

Baby Blues

by Rick Kirkman / Jerry Scott

!!!!!!

NO MORE BAKED BEANS BEFORE NURSING HAMMIE.
AGREED.

KIRKMAN & SCOTT

MOMMY?
YES?
I PUT ALL OF MY TOYS AWAY AND PUT MY DIRTY CLOTHES IN THE BASKET.
GOOD.

IF IT'S OKAY WITH YOU, I'LL VACUUM THE LIVING ROOM, FINISH THE DISHES AND KNOCK OUT A COUPLE OF LOADS OF LAUNDRY BEFORE I MAKE DINNER.

KIRKMAN & SCOTT

WHAT'S GOING ON?
MOMMY'S GIGGLING IN HER SLEEP AGAIN.
HEE! HEE! SURE! AND WASH THE PATIO WINDOWS WHILE YOU'RE AT IT...

SO, ZOE... WHAT DID YOU DO TODAY?
I PLAYED, AND THEN I COLORED.

AND THEN I PLAYED SOME MORE, AND THEN I COLORED SOME MORE...

...PLAYED, COLORED, PLAYED, PLAYED, COLORED, PLAYED, ATE A SNACK, COLORED, COLORED, PLAYED, PLAYED, WENT POTTY, COLORED, COLORED, COLORED...
I WAS LOOKING FOR A SUMMARY RATHER THAN A MINUTE-BY-MINUTE...
THEN YOU SHOULD HAVE SAID SO.
KIRKMAN & SCOTT

AIEEEEE!
DAT'S
MINE!!

NO! NO! HAMMIE!
DAT'S ZOE'S DOLLY!

MY
CAR!
MY
CAR!
KIRKMAN
& SCOTT

WHAT ARE YOU GUYS DOING?
SHARING.

NEW DAD, HUH?
YEAH. TWELVE WEEKS TODAY.
STAMPS ONLY
WAIT HERE FOR NEXT WINDOW

THAT'S GREAT. HOW'S IT GOING?
PRETTY GOOD. SHE GOES TO SLEEP EVERY TIME I PUT HER IN THE CAR.

HOW'S THE MILEAGE?
I'D SAY ABOUT TWENTY MILES TO THE NAP.
KIRKMAN & SCOTT

BLOW, ZOE.
SNIFF!

NO! DON'T SNIFF! BLOW!
BLOW!
SNIFF!

AAAUGH!
SNIFFFFXX!
KIRKMAN & SCOTT

OKAY, I'M GROSSED OUT... YOUR TURN.
AAHH... MUCH BETTER!

CAN I HAVE A DRINK OF THAT?
THIS? NO, ZOE.

THIS IS BEER. IT'S NOT FOR KIDS. IT'S ICKY.

OH.

THEN WHY ARE YOU DRINKING IT?
KIRKMAN & SCOTT

BABY BLUES

RICK KIRKMAN / JERRY SCOTT
BY

...AND ONE SPRING DAY, THE SIX YOUNG MEERKATS CAUTIOUSLY VENTURE FROM THEIR BURROW FOR THE FIRST TIME.
AAAWW... AREN'T THEY CUTE?

THOUGH TIMID AT FIRST, SOON THE MEERKATS ROMP PLAYFULLY IN THE SUN...

CRUNCH!
YAAAAGH!

MUNCH! MUNCH! MUNCH!
...WHICH IS A BAD IDEA WHEN THERE ARE HYENAS AROUND.
THE REMOTE! GET THE REMOTE!
CLICK!
CLICK!

A HYENA JUST ATE ONE OF THE BABY MEERKATS!
DON'T WORRY... I THINK THE OTHERS ARE GOING TO BE OKAY.

AS THE HUNGRY HYENA FEASTS ON HIS KILL, THE REST OF THE MEERKATS SCRAMBLE BACK TO THE DEN, WHERE THEY WOULD BE SAFE...
THERE! SEE?

GULP! GULP! GULP!
YAAAGH!

...IF A HUNGRY PYTHON HADN'T GOTTEN THERE FIRST.
I HATE NATURE!!

WHAT KIND OF NATURE SHOW IS THIS?? ALL OF THE CUTE LITTLE BABY MEERKATS ARE BEING EATEN ALIVE!
MAYBE THEY'RE TRYING TO MAKE A POINT ABOUT SURVIVAL. LET'S GIVE IT A CHANCE.
HAVING GAINED VALUABLE KNOWLEDGE ABOUT THE DANGERS OF THEIR SURROUNDINGS, THE MEERKATS TAKE TURNS KEEPING A SHARP LOOKOUT FOR OTHER PREDATORS IN THE BUSH...
SEE? WHAT DID I TELL YOU?

...UNAWARE THAT MEERKATS ARE ALSO A FAVORITE FOOD OF HAWKS,
SNATCH!
YAAAAAGH!

THAT'S IT! TURN IT OFF! I CAN'T WATCH ANOTHER CUTE LITTLE ANIMAL GET EATEN!
I THINK IT'S ABOUT OVER, ANYWAY.

YEAH... SEE? THERE'S THE GAME WARDEN COMING THROUGH THE BUSHES TO SAVE THE LAST BABY MEERKAT.
REALLY?

WELL, AT LEAST THAT'S SOME GOOD N—
CHOMP!

NO, WAIT... THAT WAS ANOTHER HYENA.
YAAAAGH!

ZOE, POLITE CHILDREN EAT WITH THEIR SPOONS AND FORKS.

THEY MUST NOT BE VERY HUNGRY!

SIGH!
WHAT'S WRONG, HONEY?

I PROMISED MYSELF THAT I WOULDN'T MAKE THE SAME MISTAKES WITH HAMMIE THAT I MADE WITH ZOE...

...AND FOR THE MOST PART, I HAVEN'T.
SO WHAT'S THE PROBLEM?

SIGH! I'M MAKING ALL NEW ONES.

BABY BLUES

BY RICK KIRKMAN / JERRY SCOTT

HAMMIE'S BOTTOM TEETH ARE REALLY GROWING IN!
THEY SURE ARE!

I THINK HE LOOKS KIND OF CUTE.
YOU DO?

I THINK HE LOOKS KIND OF LIKE SARGE IN "BEETLE BAILEY."

DO YOU THINK WE OUGHT TO TAKE HAMMIE TO A PEDIATRIC ORTHODONTIST?
WHAT?? WHY?

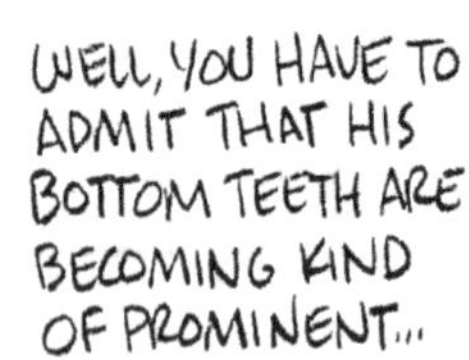

WELL, YOU HAVE TO ADMIT THAT HIS BOTTOM TEETH ARE BECOMING KIND OF PROMINENT...
SO?? WHAT'S WRONG WITH HAVING A PROMINENT FEATURE?

IT JUST DOESN'T RUN IN OUR FAMILY?
MUCH...

WHINE! WHINE! WHINE!

WHINE! WHINE! WHINE!
ZOE, IF YOU DON'T STOP WHINING, I'LL GIVE YOU SOMETHING TO WHINE ABOUT!

HUH??
IT DOESN'T MAKE ANY SENSE TO ME, EITHER, BUT IT WORKED WHEN MY MOM USED TO SAY IT.

HAVE YOU NOTICED THAT WE DON'T CARRY AROUND AS MUCH STUFF FOR HAMMIE AS WE DID WITH ZOE?

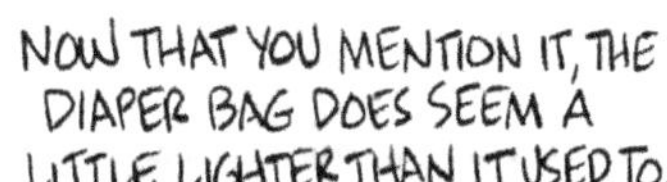

NOW THAT YOU MENTION IT, THE DIAPER BAG DOES SEEM A LITTLE LIGHTER THAN IT USED TO,

IT'S WEIRD BECAUSE IT'S ALL THE SAME STUFF... DIAPERS... WIPES... EXTRA CLOTHES—OH, WAIT! I KNOW WHAT'S MISSING!
WHAT?

THE ANXIETY.
YEAH, I GUESS THERE'S ALWAYS LESS OF THAT WITH THE SECOND BABY...

GULP!

GUESS WHO CRAWLED IN BED WITH US LAST NIGHT?

MOM! HAMMIE IS CRYING!
WANDA, HAVE YOU SEEN MY BELT?

MOM! HAMMIE BARFED!
I'M TAKING SOME OF YOUR CASH FOR LUNCH MONEY!

MOM! I NEED MORE CEREAL!
WANDA, DID YOU PICK UP MY JACKET FROM THE DRY CLEANER?

WHAT DO YOU MEAN WE DEPEND ON YOU TOO MUCH?
DADDY, TELL MOM I SPILLED MY MILK.

BABY BLUES®

RICK KIRKMAN / JERRY SCOTT BY

YOU REALLY THINK THAT WE DEPEND ON YOU TOO MUCH?
LOOK AROUND!

NOT ONLY DO I DO THE COOKING, CLEANING AND ORGANIZING AROUND HERE, I'M ALSO THE MAIN PROBLEM-SOLVER!

IF THERE'S A DISASTER, CALL MOM! IF THERE'S AN ERRAND TO BE RUN, CALL MOM! IF THERE'S A MESS TO BE CLEANED UP, AN APPOINTMENT TO KEEP, OR A DECISION TO BE MADE, CALL MOM!

WHAT DO YOU THINK WE SHOULD DO ABOUT THAT?
KIRKMAN & SCOTT

ALL I'M SAYING IS THAT I NEED A LITTLE RELIEF.
GOTCHA.

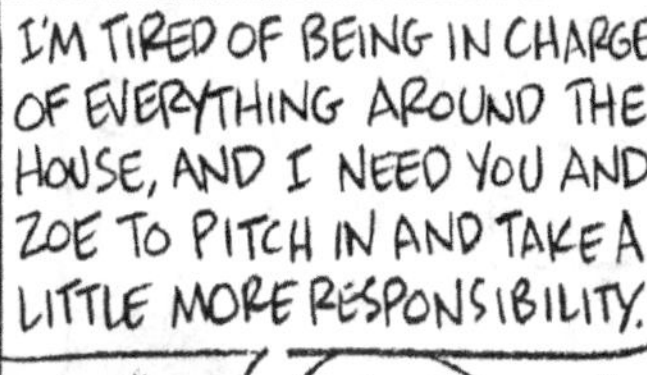

I'M TIRED OF BEING IN CHARGE OF EVERYTHING AROUND THE HOUSE, AND I NEED YOU AND ZOE TO PITCH IN AND TAKE A LITTLE MORE RESPONSIBILITY.
SAY NO MORE!

WE'LL START BY EMPTYING THE DISHWASHER FOR YOU!
THANKS, GUYS... I REALLY APPRECIATE THE—
KIRKMAN & SCOTT

WHERE DO THESE BOWLS GO?
—EFFORT.
I CAN'T REACH THE COUNTER, SO I'LL JUST PUT THESE ON THE FLOOR, OKAY?

WHEW! THE KIDS ARE FINALLY IN BED!
YEAH.
CLICK!

THINGS ARE SO NOISY AND CHAOTIC WHEN I GET HOME FROM WORK THAT I REALLY LOOK FORWARD TO THE PART OF THE EVENING WHEN I CAN SIT AND TALK TO...

...MYSELF.
ZZZZZ
KIRKMAN & SCOTT

ZOE, CAN YOU GET ME A T-SHIRT FOR HAMMIE?
SURE.

ERF! UNNH! HOLD STILL, HAMMIE!

POP!
WHEW! HAMMIE MUST REALLY BE GROWING, ZOE! THIS T-SHIRT IS ALMOST TOO SMALL.

THAT'S FUNNY... IT FITS MY TEDDY BEAR JUST FINE.
KIRKMAN & SCOTT

WATCH, DADDY, WATCH!
OKAY... I'M WATCHING!

WHUMP!

WOW! THAT WAS GREAT, ZOE! GOOD JOB! 'ATTA GIRL!

ACTUALLY, SHE JUST WANTED YOU TO SEE THE FIRST PART... THE FALLING WAS AN ACCIDENT.
OH...
THANKS A LOT, DAD.
KIRKMAN & SCOTT

LOOK! A CALLIPIDDER!

HEH-HEH! NO, ZOE... IT'S CATERPILLAR... NOT "CALLIPIDDER!"
CATERPILLAR.

CATERPILLAR... CATERPILLAR... CATERPILLAR... CATERPILLAR...
YES! THAT'S CORRECT! ABSOLUTELY CORRECT!

...AND TOTALLY UN-CUTE.
NICE GOING, MR. WEBSTER.
KIRKMAN & SCOTT

BABY BLUES

BY RICK KIRKMAN / JERRY SCOTT

DO YOU BELIEVE IN PAST LIVES?

PAST LIVES? NO, I DON'T THINK SO.

I HAVE ENOUGH TROUBLE BELIEVING THIS ONE.
MOM, HOW MANY CRAYONS ARE BABIES ALLOWED TO EAT?

DEPT. OF THE MORE THINGS CHANGE, THE MORE THEY STAY THE SAME:

COME ON... COME ON... GO TO BED SO WE CAN BE ALONE!
THEN

COME ON... COME ON... GO TO BED SO WE CAN BE ALONE!
NOW

GOTCHA!
SNAP!

YOU JUST SWATTED A FLY WITH THE DISHCLOTH?
YEAH! PRETTY GOOD, HUH?
AND YOU'RE GOING TO USE IT AGAIN?

I'M GOING TO RINSE IT OUT FIRST.
BUT STILL... IT WAS A FLY!

DON'T YOU THINK THAT'S KIND OF GROSS?
WE HAVE TWO KIDS... THAT FLY WAS PROBABLY THE UN-GROSSEST THING THIS POOR TOWEL HAS TOUCHED ALL DAY!

SINCE YOU HAVE THE WEEK OFF, MAYBE WE COULD TAKE THE KIDS TO WHISTLING MONKEY COWBOY BAND LAND FOR A DAY.
WHAT??

COME ON... IT'S ONLY A FEW HOURS AWAY.
WE COULD LEAVE EARLY IN THE MORNING, SPEND THE DAY, AND DRIVE HOME THAT EVENING.

WHAT DO YOU SAY?
NOTHING THAT COULD BE REPEATED IN MIXED COMPANY.

HOW LONG HAVE WE BEEN DRIVING?
I DON'T KNOW.

HOW MANY MILES HAVE WE GONE?
I DON'T KNOW.

MOM?...
HOW MANY POTTY STOPS SO FAR?
THIS MAKES TWENTY-SIX, BUT WHO'S COUNTING?
GAS 'N STUFF

THERE IT IS, EVERYBODY! WHISTLING MONKEY COWBOY BAND LAND!
FINALLY!
YAY!

OKAY... I HAVE THE PASSES AND THE CAMERA. LET'S GO IN AND HAVE SOME REAL FAMILY...

...FUN.
NICE SHORTS, FOUR-EYES!
WHEEE!
ENTRANCE

THIS IS NOT A GOOD SIGN...
HOW LONG DID YOU SAY YOU'VE BEEN IN LINE??
KIRKMAN & SCOTT

ON THE BRIGHT SIDE, AT LEAST WE'RE SPENDING OUR VACATION TOGETHER!
FROM THIS POINT THE WAIT IS APPROX: FOREVER
'SPLAT!'
KIRKMAN & SCOTT

IT'S HARD TO TELL, BUT...

...I THINK WE'RE ALMOST THERE!
KIRKMAN & SCOTT

I CAN'T BELIEVE WE'RE FINALLY HERE!
IT'S BEEN A LONG WAIT, BUT IT'LL BE WORTH IT JUST TO SEE THE LOOK ON ZOE'S—
MEET THE WHISTLING MONKEY COWBOY BAND!
IN PERSON

—FACE,
WAAAAAAAA!
MEET THE WHISTLING MONKEY COWBOY BAND!
CLOSED COME AGAIN TOMORROW!
WHISTLING MONKEY COWBOY BAND RAIN PONCHOS $30

SEVEN HOURS OF DRIVING... SIX HOURS OF STANDING IN LINE... $79 WORTH OF SOUVENIRS... $16 FOR PARKING... AND FOR WHAT??

THANKS, DADDY. THAT WAS FUN. I LOVE YOU.

FOR THAT.
LET'S COME AGAIN TOMORROW.

WAAAAAA!

NONONONONONO!! I WANT IT BACK!!!!!

OKAY! FINE! YOU WIN! HERE'S YOUR BALL! SHEESH!

YOU DO NICE WORK.

BABY BLUES

BY RICK KIRKMAN / JERRY SCOTT

BABY BLUES

BY RICK KIRKMAN / JERRY SCOTT

WAAAAAA!

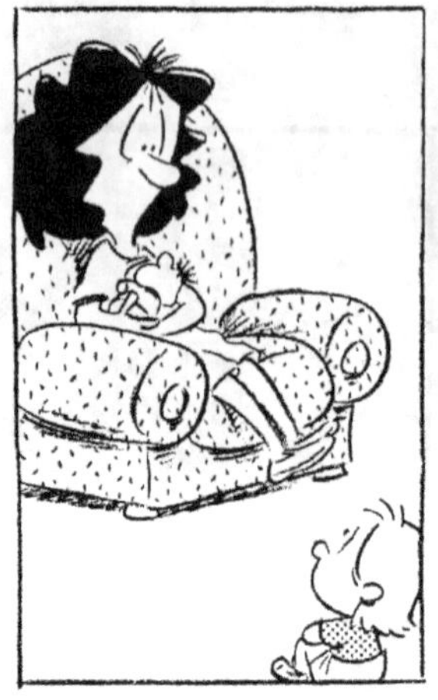

YEAH, WELL, I CAN DO A SOMERSAULT, AND YOU CAN'T!
KIRKMAN & SCOTT

WHEN I GROW UP I WANNA LIVE IN A BARBIE® HOUSE AN' HAVE A BARBIE® CAR AN' WEAR BARBIE® CLOTHES!

AN' I WANT A BARBIE® BEDROOM, AN' A BARBIE® KITCHEN, AN' A BARBIE® BATHROOM!

THAT'S ALL.?? DON'T YOU WANT MORE OUT OF LIFE, ZOE?

OH YEAH... AN' A BARBIE® BOAT!
ATTAGIRL... SHOOT FOR THE STARS!

HMMM...DIRTY DISHES NEED TO BE PUT IN THE DISHWASHER.

BUT THE DISHWASHER IS STILL FULL OF CLEAN DISHES THAT NEED TO BE PUT AWAY.

WANDA IS BUSY WITH THE KIDS, SO THERE'S ONLY ONE LOGICAL THING TO DO...
KIRKMAN & SCOTT

...PUTTER AROUND IN THE GARAGE.

WHAT ARE YOU DOING OUT HERE WHEN THE HOUSE IS SUCH A MESS??
SORTING SCREWS.

SORTING SCREWS?? THERE'S A SINK FULL OF DIRTY DISHES, A MEAL TO COOK, A HOUSE TO CLEAN, LAUNDRY TO DO, TWO KIDS THAT NEED TO BE ENTERTAINED, AND YOU DECIDE TO SORT SCREWS?? WHY??

BECAUSE THERE'S A SINK FULL OF DIRTY DISHES, A MEAL TO COOK, A HOUSE TO CLEAN, LAUNDRY TO DO...

THEY SAY THEY WANT YOU TO TELL THEM THE TRUTH, BUT THEY REALLY DON'T.
KIRKMAN & SCOTT

YEAH. OKAY. BYE.
WHO WAS THAT?

SOME CHARITY SOLICITING DONATIONS...
WHAT DID YOU SAY?

I TOLD THEM THAT WE HAVE ONE INCOME, TWO KIDS, A MORTGAGE, CAR PAYMENT, CREDIT CARD BILLS, AND FUTURE COLLEGE TUITION TO WORRY ABOUT, SO THINGS ARE REALLY TIGHT RIGHT NOW.
KIRKMAN & SCOTT

I HOPE THEY UNDERSTAND...
THEY'RE DROPPING OFF FIFTY BUCKS AND AN OLD SOFA.

HI, HAMMIEEE! ARE YOU ALL DWESSED? HUH?

YOU LOOK SOOO NICE! YES YOU DO!
I'M GLAD YOU LIKE HAMMIE'S OUTFIT, ZOE... IT USED TO BE YOURS.

DID I WEAR BOY CLOTHES, OR IS HE WEARING GIRL CLOTHES?
KIRKMAN & SCOTT

BABY BLUES

BY RICK KIRKMAN / JERRY SCOTT

WAAAAAAA!
MOMMY, HAMMIE IS CRYING.
SO I HEAR. DO YOU KNOW WHY?

WAAAAAAAA!
I THINK HE WANTS HIS PACIFIER.
REALLY?

WHAT MAKES YOU THINK SO?
KIRKMAN & SCOTT

HI, ZOE. WHAT ARE YOU WATCHING?
TV.

I KNOW IT'S TV... I MEAN, WHAT KIND OF A SHOW ARE YOU WATCHING?
A TV SHOW.

I KNOW THAT! BUT WHICH TV SHOW IS IT?
THIS ONE.

IS THAT ALL YOU WANTED TO KNOW?
KIRKMAN & SCOTT

BOO!
DARRYL!
EEEEK!

WAAAA! DADDY SCARED ME!
I'M SORRY... I WAS JUST—
WHY DON'T YOU PICK ON SOMEBODY YOUR OWN SIZE?

SNIF!

DO IT AGAIN!
KIRKMAN & SCOTT

DAD! DAD! DAD! DAD! DAD! DAD! DAD! DAD!
WHA-HUH?

WHAT IS IT, ZOE? WHAT'S WRONG?
MOMMY SAID TO COME IN HERE VERY QUIETLY AND SEE IF YOU WERE STILL ASLEEP, AND I DID IT ALL BY MYSELF!

ARE YOU PROUD OF ME?
I'M SOMETHING, BUT I DON'T THINK "PROUD" DESCRIBES IT.
KIRKMAN & SCOTT

www.ingramcontent.com/pod-product-compliance
Lightning Source LLC
Chambersburg PA
CBHW080945010726

47382CB00038B/510